You can't get too much Efrem Smith. He has the voice of a prophet and the heart of a pastor. This book is nothing short of an invitation to follow the revolutionary Jesus. It's a call to live in ways that don't compute, to fight with weapons that do not kill, and to love in a way that confounds the world.

SHANE CLAIBORNE
Author and activist

Efrem Smith has got it right. This *is* an upside-down world—for Christians as well. We cling to differences that divide us instead of to Christ, who unites us; we're known in the public sphere for what we're against rather than what we're for; and we're more likely to pursue the American dream than join Jesus' revolution of radical love. God can't use us in this condition. *Killing Us Softly* is an eloquent reflection on what it means to die to self in order to live right side up as Christ's ambassadors in a broken world.

RICHARD STEARNS
President of World Vision US and author of *The Hole in Our Gospel*

We need to stop peddling a convenient and palatable version of Christianity. To invite people to Christ without discipleship is an oxymoron. This is precisely why *Killing Us Softly* is so important and timely. This is a powerful, biblical, bold, prophetic, and yet pastoral reminder of the call of discipleship.

REV. EUGENE CHO
Pastor, humanitarian, and author of *Overrated*

In a Western Christian world that is often enamored of outward appearance, upward mobility, and the acquisition of power, Efrem Smith is here to proclaim that there is another way—one that leads to true freedom and a commitment to justice. I love this book because Efrem recognizes that in order to do good work in this broken world, we must first examine our hearts, experiences, and identities. To this end, Efrem offers a concise spirituality and set of practices that form us to transform this world. Efrem is one of the most innovative evangelicals leading at the intersection of justice and spirituality. I do not take his words lightly.

CHRISTENA CLEVELAND, PHD
Associate professor of the practice of reconciliation, Duke Divinity School, and author of *Disunity in Christ*

Killing Us Softly provides a compelling vision of transformation for our fallen world. The reminder that through Christ all things are being turned right side up and conformed to his splendor is especially hopeful for those of us who are called to live and minister in vulnerable communities. Biblical. Challenging. Hopeful.

NOEL CASTELLANOS
President of Christian Community Development Association and author of *Where the Cross Meets the Street*

killing us softly

Reborn in the Upside-Down Image of God

EFREM SMITH

NAVPRESS

*A NavPress resource published in alliance
with Tyndale House Publishers, Inc.*

NavPress is the publishing ministry of The Navigators, an international Christian organization and leader in personal spiritual development. NavPress is committed to helping people grow spiritually and enjoy lives of meaning and hope through personal and group resources that are biblically rooted, culturally relevant, and highly practical.

For more information, visit www.NavPress.com.

Copyright © 2017 by Efrem Smith. All rights reserved.

A NavPress resource published in alliance with Tyndale House Publishers, Inc.

NAVPRESS and the NAVPRESS logo are registered trademarks of NavPress, The Navigators, Colorado Springs, CO. *TYNDALE* is a registered trademark of Tyndale House Publishers, Inc. Absence of ® in connection with marks of NavPress or other parties does not indicate an absence of registration of those marks.

The Team:
Don Pape, Publisher
David Zimmerman, Acquiring Editor, Development Editor
Mark Anthony Lane II, Designer

Cover illustration of flower type copyright © Ian Barnard/Creative Market. All rights reserved.

Cover photograph of grunge background copyright © 123creativecom/Creative Market. All rights reserved.

Author photo by World Impact and Travis Silva, copyright © 2016. All rights reserved.

For information about special discounts for bulk purchases, please contact Tyndale House Publishers at csresponse@tyndale.com or call 800-323-9400.

Library of Congress Cataloging-in-Publication Data
Names: Smith, Efrem (Efrem D.), 1969- author.
Title: Killing us softly : reborn in the upside-down image of God / Efrem Smith.
Description: Colorado Springs, CO : NavPress, resource published in alliance with Tyndale House Publishers, Inc., [2017] | Description based on print version record and CIP data provided by publisher; resource not viewed.
Identifiers: LCCN 2016048613 (print) | LCCN 2016038960 (ebook) | ISBN 9781631465239 (Apple) | ISBN 9781631465215 (E-Pub) | ISBN 9781631465222 (Kindle) | ISBN 9781631465208 (softcover)
Subjects: LCSH: Christian life. | Identity (Psychology)—Religious aspects—Christianity.
Classification: LCC BV4501.3 (print) | LCC BV4501.3 .S65165 2017 (ebook) | DDC 248.4—dc23
LC record available at https://urldefense.proofpoint.com/v2/url?u=https-3A__lccn.loc.gov_20
16048613&d=DQIFAg&c=6BNjZEuL_DAs869UxGis0g&r=ZlF6A1J_SMm9xAyjgyDor34CB-fqQR
araBLNVSdnrVo&m=FARMZtFHgpLmtWweU6XYmUvoFerQP1zbtND4NaGdni0&s=c2qTjOvli7
ZPT3-2KkEqU6ph-3aj7Qv3qo_-lyHjfb0&e=

Printed in the United States of America

23	22	21	20	19	18	17
7	6	5	4	3	2	1

To my father and mother,
Forice and Sandra Smith

Contents

Introduction

I'M SITTING IN THE SANCTUARY of a black church in the small town of Bosco, Louisiana, near the city of Monroe in the northern part of the state. This is where my father, Forice Smith, was born and raised. I'm in my early teens. I'm sitting with my father, my mother Sandra, and my younger brother Tramaine in this small church called Cuba Missionary Baptist. Singing, shouting, prayers, and amens fill the air. With smiles and laughs the people agree with the testimonies that are given. The pastor preaches a sermon that includes a climactic declaration that the grave couldn't hold Jesus and that through his resurrection we can all find a home in glory. Many folks begin clapping.

What a service this was. The fact that I still remember it signifies how meaningful it was to me. But this was not a Sunday morning worship experience. This was actually the funeral service for my grandfather, Fred Smith.

"Grand Daddy Fred" had been a dedicated deacon

in this small country church. His faith in Christ had a tremendous impact on me as a kid. There were a few summers when my parents would pack up the car and we would drive from Minneapolis, Minnesota, all the way into the Deep South. Those hot summers provided opportunities to play with my southern cousins, sit at the feet of elders who had lived through Jim Crow segregation, and eat my grandmother Mary's made-from-scratch biscuits just about every morning for breakfast. I also remember Grand Daddy Fred sitting on the porch early each morning, reading the Bible out loud. My brother Tramaine, cousin Keisha, and I would wake up most mornings to his voice reading the Word of God. Most of the time he was a very quiet man, so many times when I heard his voice, it was Scripture that was being spoken. Because of his witness, I had no trouble believing that when he died he was going to be in heaven.

I was sad when Grand Daddy Fred died. I cried on my mother's shoulder during the funeral. But I also found myself moved by the call of the pastor to celebrate his death, knowing that he was with the One he spoke of so often when he sat on the porch reading the Bible out loud.

I came to understand something unique about black church funerals. Many African American pastors encourage those mourning the loss of their loved one to see this service not as a funeral but as a "home-going." I have heard this term all my life. I can't remember a time when I have attended a funeral service led by an African American pastor when this term wasn't used.

By speaking in terms of "home-going," the pastor is not trying to take away from the reality of the pain and sorrow that family and friends are feeling from losing someone who meant so much to them. The purpose of positioning this event as a home-going service is to remind those mourning that if the person was Christian, they are now in a better place. It's appropriate to mourn but allow room in your heart to celebrate as well.

I have been to black home-going services where sorrow and mourning share space with "Hallelujah!" and "Praise God!" Songs of lament share space with songs of celebration. Sounds of wailing are mixed with shouts of joy. The pastor encourages the congregation to remember that the deceased is now face to face with their Lord and Savior. They have transitioned to the heavenly realm, where there is no more pain and no more sorrow. Though the death of a beloved child of God brings pain to those of us still in the earthly realm, our loved one has now transitioned into eternity.

This approach to the funeral in the black church finds its beginnings within the context of slavery. The black church began as an invisible, underground church. I often hear evangelicals speak of underground churches in the Middle East or in parts of Asia or Eastern Europe—places where Christians have to gather in secret because their coming together as a church body is illegal. Well, the black church in the United States began as just such an underground and illegal gathering. Black slaves would retreat late at night into the woods of the Deep South to pray, sing, and hear a more liberating take on the Bible. They would create what would become known as spirituals. Many of these spirituals were contextualized hymns, centered around freedom. Not knowing whether they would ever experience freedom in this world, these people would sing and preach about the freedom they would one day experience in heaven. This makes sense of a chorus such as "Swing low, sweet chariot, coming for to carry me home." There was a belief that God could come and deliver them into heaven, a place of freedom and direct relationship with a liberating God.

It is within the upside-down, oppressive, and unjust system of American slavery that an organic theology of death as transition into freedom is developed. This could also have been something of a coping mechanism for slaves, a way of addressing the fear of death. Death for the black slave could very well have been seen as better than life.

Christian theology in general does point to death not being an end so much as a transition. Death brings forth the opportunity to experience freedom and direct relationship with God in fullness. Christ tells his followers in the Gospels that he goes to prepare a place for them. The Promised Land into which God led the Hebrews in the Old Testament has been replaced in Christ by an eternal Kingdom. Death is defeated in Christ because death is not the end for the Christian. Death is not to be feared by the Christian.

This book is about death. But it's not about physically dying; it's about *spiritually* dying. Embracing death is a way of understanding a key element of Christian formation. Dying spiritually can be a way to experience our decreasing so that God might increase in our lives. Just as physical death for the Christian is the transition into a deeper and eternal experience of the Kingdom of God—we will see our God face to face—there is a spiritual death that can lead us into greater intimacy with God and a deeper discovery of our life mission *right now*.

When we became Christians, we died to our old selves and became new creations. The Christian life is about the journey of experiencing that death to the old self and becoming a new self. Physical death is our entrance into the Kingdom of God; embracing a life of spiritual dying is our participation in the Kingdom's entering into this sinful and broken world. To serve as ambassadors of reconciliation and advancers of the Kingdom, we must be willing to die.

Death is not a comfortable topic for me. Though

I anticipate being in eternity with my God one day, I also struggle, as I enter my late forties, with thinking about my death. I can only imagine that the moment that I start to enter my death will truly test everything that I believe about being a Christian. Similarly, embracing spiritual death has not been easy for me. But I am experiencing more and more how liberating it is. I am allowing God to do surgery on my soul—to kill me, certainly, but to do so softly, lovingly—so that I might die to the upside-down world we find ourselves in, and be empowered to live as a right-side-up child of God. I am living in the messiness of God removing things in me that are not of him so that my life might reflect him more each day.

This book is an invitation to enter into this journey of being killed softly by God's steadfast love and grace, that we might be living vehicles of God's love, truth, grace, justice, and transformation.

FOR REFLECTION AND DISCUSSION

Think about the funerals and home-going celebrations you've experienced in your life. How has death impacted you?

Recall a loved one whose life pointed you to the Kingdom of God. How were you blessed by his or her life?

1

LIVING IN A
BIZARRO WORLD

I LOVE SUPERHERO MOVIES. In the past few years I have seen *The Avengers, X-Men, Guardians of the Galaxy, The Fantastic Four, Spider-Man, Ant-Man,* and *Captain America: Civil War* leap from the pages of comic books to the film screen. I have seen these films multiple times in theaters, on DVD, and on cable television. Not to be outdone by these characters from the Marvel Comics universe, DC Comics superheroes have made it to film as well, with heroes such as Batman and Superman and, I hope, many more in the future. I really love superhero movies.

This love for superheroes goes back to my child-hood in Minneapolis, Minnesota. In the summer months I would meet my friends on the corner at the end of our block. We would sit on the sidewalk, reading, comparing, and trading our *Thor, Spider-Man, Batman,* and *Superman* comics. There was one comic series that was my favorite; I still have some of those comics today. It's a Superman comic series called *Bizarro World*.

Bizarro is an upside-down world—so upside-down that there is a villain on Bizarro World who looks just like Superman. Our world is threatened by Bizarro World, so Superman decides to sacrifice himself, leaving our world to confront Bizarro Superman on his home planet.

To go with this storyline, you have to believe that for the most part, things on planet Earth are good. Where we live there is peace and harmony, families are stable, and communities are flourishing. Our planet is fine; it's Bizarro World that is backward and broken.

But the truth is, we live in Bizarro World. Sure, we can point to examples of good communities, stable families, and peace and harmony here and there. But if we're honest, there are far too many signs that our reality is Bizarro.

Violence as the primary means of solving conflict.

Continued racial strife and tensions.

Broken families and fatherless homes.

Human beings sold into slavery.

Poverty and disease plaguing whole nations.

Yes, if we're honest, we live in an upside-down world. From individual people to institutions and societal systems, there is brokenness and backward-ness all around us. And like the Bizarro World of the comics, the upside-down world we inhabit seems, to the untrained eye, to be right side up.

As Christians, we follow a God who promises a very different kind of world. What is our responsibility to our broken and upside-down world? How do we dis-cover our purpose in it?

It's one thing to admit the reality of the upside-down world; it's another to know how Christ wants us to engage it. It begins with a deeper understanding of the ultimate heroic one, Jesus Christ.

When Christ, the Son of God, left the heavenly realms to confront our upside-down world, he came in human form. The Scriptures tell us why he came and what he came to do: "For God so loved the world, that he gave his only Son, that whoever believes in him should not perish but have eternal life" (John 3:16).

Christ gave us a picture of what this world could look like if it was set right side up again. When Christ gave mobility to the paralyzed, when a diseased woman touched his clothes and was healed, when he raised a girl from the dead, and when he ate with sin-ners, he was demonstrating the Kingdom of God—the world set right.

In his teaching, Christ declared that the Kingdom of God was at hand. You would think the prospect of such a world would be received with joy, but his declarations and demonstrations led him to the cross. Christ died for this Bizarro world. And in so doing, he demonstrated finally and emphatically that Bizarro lives matter to God.

Because Christ died for us and, in a particularly Bizarro moment, rose again from the grave and conquered death for us, we who embrace him as Lord and Savior can experience our lives being turned right side up. And one day he will return to our world and finally, emphatically turn it right side up. On that day we will experience a new heaven and a new earth— a world with no tears, no pain, no brokenness, no backwardness—no death.

Until then, we continue to live in an upside-down reality. We have to figure out how to do that well, and what our role is as right-side-up people in an upside-down world.

We who have joined with the Kingdom of God live in an uncomfortable place. Freed by Christ's sacrifice, we nevertheless continue to occupy systems, institutions, and even beliefs calibrated to an upside-down world. Our friends and neighbors have grown accustomed to living upside-down. The world is killing them, but it's doing so in a way that feels simply like normal life.

The church seems to be divided when it comes to understanding what it means to live in this sinful and broken world. Some Christians see the challenge as individual sinners in need of being saved from their individual sins. Others see the challenge as sinful systems of injustice and oppression. Still others see the challenge as entirely supernatural: Our battle is focused entirely on Satan, God's archenemy.

They're all right—to a point. Our problem is that our world is upside-down: Individuals are plagued with sin, systems and structures are steeped in sin, and Satan is engaged in a protracted battle to keep the world broken by sin. We need this holistic understanding of our challenge so that we can have a more biblical approach to engaging it for transformation.

BROKEN LIVES

Whether we realize it or not, our broken lives are killing us from the inside. We may not feel as if we are dying on the inside, but we are. We are being separated from the wonderful and eternal person that God has created us each to be. Sin is a silent killer seeking to strip us of our true identity and purpose. Sin can lead someone to live in a continual state of anger, hatred, pride, arrogance, low self-esteem, abandonment, prejudice, unforgiveness, or selfishness.

Sin and the broken life it engenders in us convince us on the inside that we are less than average, that we will never amount to anything. Sin can be a death sentence on a person's life. Sin can also lead to a person thinking more of themselves than they should, producing a sort of self-worship. Whether by thinking that we are less than God created us to be or by living as gods unto ourselves, living in sin and being impacted by sinful forces and structures is a slow death leading to eternal death. Sin causes us to live life on a death march.

But sin does more than just kill *us*. It also seeks to kill others *through* us. Sinful and broken people who are slowly dying on the inside can pass their spiritually toxic death sentence on to others. Sinful people collectively build broken families, governments, systems, institutions, and communities. This causes sin to go from killing a person to killing whole people groups, entire communities, and potentially a nation. This is what oppression ultimately looks like.

This killing process can look like a father who abandons his wife and child. How did he arrive at such a decision? Is he simply a sinful individual, a bad father and husband? Or is there more going on?

Considered holistically, the answer is not simple. We're dealing with someone who is dying on the inside. His own sinful behavior, combined with the sinful and broken systems surrounding the community where he lives—oppression from within and from without—leads him to an act of betrayal. Though he has applied for jobs he is more than qualified for, he is denied in every instance. Businesses have abandoned his neighborhood where just a few years earlier there were plenty of jobs. He feels like less than a man now. Though you can't totally blame his choice on systems, the oppressive systems around him have made it difficult for him to see himself as someone made in the image of God. Some days when he should be working, he finds himself just walking down the street. Some of the retired people in the community and even some of the police officers look at him as if he is a threat to the community, but he's just wandering the streets instead of working a full-time job somewhere. He is softly dying and doesn't even know how to communicate the state of his soul. Gradually his despair turns to anger. He begins to treat his wife differently. There are regular arguments that fill the home on a nightly basis. And eventually he leaves.

So, slowly dying, he makes a choice that extends his dying to others. His choice to leave creates bitterness toward men within his wife, who is now raising a child on her own. She carries anger in her heart, believing that she will never be able to trust another man again. Her pride might not show it, but sin through a broken relationship is killing her on the inside. Meanwhile, her son is now growing up without a father. This broken relationship leads to a boy growing into manhood while struggling with abandonment. Sin showing up in people, systems, and relationships is deadly indeed.

I have been a pastor, mostly in the urban context, for a little over twenty-five years. I have encountered many people who are dying on the inside as they attempt to navigate their sinful lives and this upside-down, sinful world. I have sat with some who in tears come to a place of recognizing their broken lives. What is more challenging are those who don't realize that sin is slowly killing them. This makes sinful choices and systems seem like right choices and just systems. They are so conditioned by this Bizarro world we live in that they have accepted the upside-down world as just right for them. The upside-down, sinful world is experienced by them as right side up.

Sin is both an individual and a systemic reality. There are some people who have no problem seeing how sin shows up in an individual, begins to kill that person, and affects their relationships, passing on spiritual death. They have a harder time believing that sinful systems, institutions, and structures also can play an oppressive role. But it is sinful and broken people who build our systems and institutions. Sin is just that deadly.

Sin impacts the very core of our being. We are born with broken hearts and broken minds. Sin causes us to deceive ourselves, to think that we can achieve a good life under this death sentence.

We were originally created to bear God's image, to work in relationship with our Creator, to steward

God's creation and fill the world with the glory of God (Genesis 1:26-28). God created us right side up. Sin altered this. Sin causes us to fear, to doubt, and to mistrust God's truth. We are led to question God's intentions for us, isolating ourselves from God and the intimate relationship that would be available to us.

Our broken and sinful lives are directly tied to this broken relationship with God. The disruption of the relationship between God and those made in God's own image turned all of creation upside down. God, of course, remains right side up. So God seems strange to us, and the things of this broken world seem safer. Upside-down people are tempted to worship the upside-down creations of God rather than the right-side-up God.

God, of course, cannot affirm an upside-down world or the upside-down logic that goes with it. Neither can he excuse the people who bear his image for their rejection of him.

> What can be known about God is plain to them, because God has shown it to them. For his invisible attributes, namely, his eternal power and divine nature, have been clearly perceived, ever since the creation of the world, in the things that have been made. So they are without excuse. For although they knew God, they did not honor him as God or give thanks

to him, but they became futile in their thinking,
and their foolish hearts were darkened.
Claiming to be wise, they became fools, and
exchanged the glory of the immortal God for
images resembling mortal man and birds and
animals and creeping things.

Therefore God gave them up in the lusts of
their hearts to impurity, to the dishonoring of
their bodies among themselves, because they
exchanged the truth about God for a lie and
worshiped and served the creature rather than
the Creator, who is blessed forever! Amen.
Romans 1:19-25

The upside-down life is an idolatrous life—our
hearts and worship turned away from God toward
other things. This leads to dishonorable passions (the
upside-down heart) and debased thinking (the upside-
down mind). When a person is inordinately passionate about material things—such as houses, cars, and
money, or even other people—they are exchanging
the glory of the immortal God for other things. This is
worldly passion, evidence of an upside-down heart.
Debased thinking privileges the philosophies and
ideologies of this world over and against the wisdom, revelation, and knowledge of God. When we put
worldly logic over *logos* (the Word of God, God as the
living Word), we elevate the ways of an upside-down

world over God. What can seem like signs of success, power, contentment, and happiness in the upside-down world can actually be the very things holding us captive, killing us. It's not that success, influence, and power are in and of themselves bad things. It's how those things, in the context of a Bizarro world, can take hold of us.

I was able to see an example of this when I planted a church in inner-city Minneapolis in 2003. Though the Sanctuary Covenant was planted in a predominantly African American and urban community, the church grew pretty quickly not only in number but also in diversity. The diversity extended well beyond race: There were social workers worshiping in the same space as professional athletes, corporate executives, politicians, and homeless people. I have to admit that I was both surprised and excited when I began to see the number of corporate executives joining the church. As a young urban pastor, I desired to see the church become a self-sustaining, transformative force of evangelism, discipleship, and community development in our under-resourced urban setting. Seeing families who were college-educated and professional join the church built a type of security in me that we could become the type of church I envisioned. I hate to admit it, but I stereotyped people by class early on in my church-planting experience: I saw the poor as the people we would reach, equip, and empower, and the well-resourced as those who would assist me in that endeavor.

I remember the afternoon I went to visit an executive vice president of a Fortune 500 company who had recently decided to join the church with his family. I went to meet him with the intention of sharing the vision I had for church growth, deeper commitment to community development, and a potential site for a church building. I was hoping he would be inspired by all of this and give financially to it. As I sat in his office and began to share passionately about where our church could go, I noticed that he had a strange look on his face. Was I doing a bad job of communicating? Did I need to go to a seminar on how to present vision to corporate executives?

He looked at me and said that he was hoping that I had come to meet with *him*—not to talk about the church but to talk about *him*. He began to share with me about the pressures of his responsibilities, the various temptations and attacks that come your way in a position like his. He shared about the struggles of trying to balance the high demands of his job with being a husband and father. He shared in a very transparent way about how guys like him were dying inside. "I was looking forward to meeting with you because I really need a pastor, and I need the community of other Christian men. You shouldn't assume guys like me are doing fine because of our titles, wealth, and influence."

I felt ashamed in my soul. I had gone through my life up until that point assuming that people like him had great lives. Sure, I believed that they needed a relationship with God through Jesus Christ and that they needed to live the life of a disciple-maker, but I had been conditioned to believe, based on their success in this world, that their lives were already right side up.

This man's transparency totally dismantled my thinking. I had to come to terms with a faulty belief system that I had been carrying around. Because I grew up in a blue-collar urban family setting, I had grown to believe that the right-side-up life was built on achievement and success. As a kid, I dreamed of going to college, getting a great-paying job, owning a nice house, and driving a luxury car. Because I sensed a call to ministry my senior year in college, I walked away from this dream in my early twenties. Following "the call of God" into ministry was honorable, I believed, but it included sacrificing the dream of success I had.

I still, however, continued to believe on some level that the ultimate sign of living right side up was "the successful life" according to the American Dream. Moving up, the pursuit of prosperity in and of itself, was the right-side-up life I had adopted in my thinking and sacrificed for my call. I looked up to "successful" people.

Moreover, because I began my ministry career in the

urban parachurch context (such as Hospitality House and the Fellowship of Christian Athletes), I relied on financial donors to raise my salary. During the twelve years I spent as an urban parachurch youth pastor, I spent a lot of time going to successful marketplace Christians to raise money. I carried this mind-set into how I approached successful people as a church planter and pastor. My focus was on their success and ability to financially support my ministry. They themselves weren't my focus. I never thought that they might be dying inside.

I'm grateful for the meeting I had in the office of this successful executive who was willing to bare his soul. Through him I connected with other business executives within the church who were themselves struggling with the challenges of our upside-down world. We started a group that met monthly for breakfast, prayer, Bible study, and fellowship. Our families began to connect on a regular basis.

In our monthly meetings, a different type of dying on the inside began taking place. God was doing something on the inside of us, so that we would be empowered through the Holy Spirit to live right-side up at home and at work. Around the table at our local diner, we explored the contrast between dying in the soul from the pressures of the world, and dying to self in order to discover more deeply what it means to be the beloved child of God.

In order to do this, we had to be willing to wrestle with how deadly sin could be—even after making the commitment to follow Christ. Sin is self-perpetuating, slowly and silently killing every person who refuses to acknowledge his or her sins and repent. Even those who are experiencing some level of joy, happiness, and peace in their upside-down lives are slowly dying. Living with sin in this way is a slow death—so slow that we think it's normal life.

But individual sin and struggle is not the only sign that we live in a broken and upside-down world. Our sin works its way out of us to do its deathly work on our relationships. We also must acknowledge the upside-down impact of our broken world on our relationships.

BROKEN RELATIONSHIPS

Soon after sin entered into our world through the first man and woman, brokenness disrupted the relationship between two of their sons, Cain and Abel.

> In the course of time Cain brought to the LORD an offering of the fruit of the ground, and Abel also brought of the firstborn of his flock and of their fat portions. And the LORD had regard for Abel and his offering, but for Cain and his offering he had no regard. So Cain was very angry, and his face fell. The LORD said to Cain,

"Why are you angry, and why has your face fallen? If you do well, will you not be accepted? And if you do not do well, sin is crouching at the door. Its desire is for you, but you must rule over it."

Cain spoke to Abel his brother. And when they were in the field, Cain rose up against his brother Abel and killed him.
Genesis 4:3-8

Could it be that sin caused Cain to believe his identity was strictly in the fruit of his labor? Once we've abandoned our identity in God, upside-down people begin to look for our identity in what we produce. God himself anticipated this in his judgment of Adam: "Cursed is the ground because of you; in pain you shall eat of it all the days of your life" (Genesis 3:17). The outcome of sin was that Adam was being ruled by the very things he was supposed to have dominion over. The world had been turned upside down. His son Cain adapted accordingly, basing his identity on the very things he was supposed to have dominion over.

This broken pursuit of acceptance breeds insecurity. We compete with the people around us for acceptance. For Cain, that competition led to him killing his own brother. But even before we read about the broken relationship between Cain and Abel, we see brokenness between Adam and Eve and between Eve and her children at the moment of childbirth.

To the woman he said,

"I will surely multiply your pain in childbearing;
    in pain you shall bring forth children.
Your desire shall be for your husband,
    and he shall rule over you.
Genesis 3:16

The simple act of bringing life into this world—which God had instructed Adam and Eve to do—put pain between the mother and her child. One could argue that the devaluing of life in the womb is a direct result of the broken and upside-down relationships that came from the Fall.

There are so many tragic and sinful examples of broken relationships. Within the family structure we see fatherlessness and divorce, authoritarian relationships and abuse. But broken relationships aren't limited to the home: We see racism, tribalism, and sexism turning relationships upside down at a culture-wide level. These can manifest in truly horrific ways, from rape to human trafficking to acts of terror. It is heartbreaking, the level of unforgiveness, selfishness, hatred, prejudice, and jealousy that exists between human beings. It is tragic, the consequences of our world being turned upside down.

BROKEN SYSTEMS AND INSTITUTIONS

If it wasn't enough that this upside-down world is marked by broken lives and broken relationships, upside-down people in upside-down relationships eventually organize themselves into upside-down structures, systems, and institutions. We see many examples in Scripture of fallen humanity building structures to their own glory over an all-powerful God. We see the beginnings of this in the attempt to build the tower of Babel.

> Now the whole earth had one language and the same words. And as people migrated from the east, they found a plain in the land of Shinar and settled there. And they said to one another, "Come, let us make bricks, and burn them thoroughly." And they had brick for stone, and bitumen for mortar. Then they said, "Come, let us build ourselves a city and a tower with its top in the heavens, and let us make a name for ourselves, lest we be dispersed over the face of the whole earth."
> *Genesis 11:1-4*

An upside-down people decide to make a name for themselves, the dysfunction of Cain on a system-wide scale. God scattered them to foil this upside-down strategy based on upside-down thinking, but we'll see it again soon enough.

In the book of Exodus, we find another example of upside-down thinking. Pharaoh enslaves the Israelites out of fear of their population growth. The Israelites cry out to the one true God for deliverance, and God responds by demanding that this system be turned right side up.

> I have surely seen the affliction of my people
> who are in Egypt and have heard their cry
> because of their taskmasters. I know their
> sufferings, and I have come down to deliver
> them out of the hand of the Egyptians and
> to bring them up out of that land to a good
> and broad land, a land flowing with milk
> and honey, to the place of the Canaanites,
> the Hittites, the Amorites, the Perizzites, the
> Hivites, and the Jebusites. And now behold, the
> cry of the people of Israel has come to me, and
> I have also seen the oppression with which the
> Egyptians oppress them.
> *Exodus 3:7-9*

In the wilderness God makes a covenant with the now-liberated Israelites and establishes a code for how they should live in relationship with God and with one another. But the insecurity of an upside-down world causes the Israelites to seek their own way. While waiting for Moses to come down from the mountain with new instructions from God, the whole multitude of people participate in the upside-down act of idolatry.

> When the people saw that Moses delayed to come down from the mountain, the people gathered themselves together to Aaron and said to him, "Up, make us gods who shall go before us. As for this Moses, the man who brought us out of the land of Egypt, we do not know what has become of him." So Aaron said to them, "Take off the rings of gold that are in the ears of your wives, your sons, and your daughters, and bring them to me." So all the people took off the rings of gold that were in their ears and brought them to Aaron. And he received the gold from their hand and fashioned it with a graving tool and made a golden calf.
> *Exodus 32:1-4*

Even when we experience God's deliverance, it's still possible to participate in upside-down corporate practices. Today, we are surrounded by broken systems and institutions: government systems, school systems, corporate systems, and economic systems. My experiences as an urban youth pastor and church planter provided me with an up-close understanding of how such broken systems and institutions work. While I was an urban youth pastor, I was also a high school basketball coach, and I watched as public school superintendents came and went in short periods of time. School board meetings seemed to be more about political-party agendas than urban children and their families. The school board would decide to close a school, and then a few years later we would have schools that were overcrowded. The schools in predominantly African American and lower-income neighborhoods were less resourced than those in predominantly white and upper-middle-income neighborhoods. Our public school system had a board and superintendent who were at odds, a teachers union that wasn't happy, complex political dynamics, and disparities in how funds were allocated. Some of the schools in our lower-income neighborhoods began to close or become alternative schools. Some parents in those neighborhoods began to send their children to private or suburban schools. Tax dollars often followed those children, contributing to a broken economic system.

I began to realize that in order to understand what was going on in the public schools and how that was impacting urban youth and families to whom I was connected as a youth pastor and basketball coach, I had to learn more about our educational, political, and economic systems. These broken systems were directly connected to struggling individuals, families, and institutions. Because I also had grown up in this community, I came to the understanding that there had been something going on in my city systemically for a long time. The city I grew up in, the city that was home to the young people I pastored, was upside-down.

With a team of mostly volunteers I sought to develop a right-side-up youth ministry that not only focused on evangelism and discipleship *to* urban youth, but also engaged broken systems and structures *on behalf of* urban youth. I realized eventually that my calling at the time was not just to minister to urban youth but also to train both youth and adults to seek to transform the upside-down systems and institutions that young people and their families were navigating on a daily basis. This kind of commitment would take a life of dying to self in order to discover a more revolutionary purpose.

When I was the youth pastor at Park Avenue United Methodist Church in South Minneapolis, I actually named our youth ministry the Park Avenue Youth Revolution. We were committed to being a ministry that raised up young heroes for God in an upside-down reality. I believed that if God could use young people in the Bible such as David, Esther, and Jeremiah to confront and transform the upside-down realities of idolatry, exile, and war, then surely God could use our urban youth as change agents in our upside-down world today.

This is not just a call for youth ministry leaders. Parents, coaches, teachers, and volunteer tutors who are committed to the right-side-up life in the Kingdom of God can equip young people as heroes for God in an upside-down world. Young people today must be conscious of, and empowered to deal with, the sinful and upside-down systems that are slowly and silently killing us.

An upside-down world organizes itself to function as effectively and efficiently as possible. This is the ultimate extrapolation of our individual brokenness—personal sin metastasizing in sinful systems that foster further personal and relational sin. It's a Bizarro trinity, a twisted version of God's vision for humanity. No wonder the world is killing us—it's not the world we were made for.

FOR REFLECTION AND DISCUSSION

What examples of broken systems and institutions have you observed in your everyday life? What impact have you seen their brokenness have on individuals and families?

What role does your faith play in how you relate to the people in your community? What role does faith play in how you interact with institutions and other cultural forces where you live?

2

THE UPSIDE-DOWN WORLD AND THE RIGHT-SIDE-UP REMNANT

THE COMMUNITY I grew up in changed a lot over the time I lived there. My parents bought their first home when I was just four years old. The neighborhood was predominantly white and middle/working class. Over time, more and more white families moved out of the neighborhood—not all of them, of course, but enough for me to notice that things were drastically changing. I began to wonder whether they were moving out because my family had moved in.

As the community became more African American, Asian, and Hispanic, more and more white-owned businesses left the community. Eventually even some of the black-owned businesses began to leave. In their place came churches and nonprofit community-service organizations. Of course I am not against churches and nonprofit organizations, but they don't tend to create jobs or otherwise bring economic growth to the neighborhood. As the businesses left, my community began to struggle financially.

When you live in a broken community, your life can turn upside down. I was fortunate: I was raised in the church, and my hard-working parents instilled strong values and character within me. There were many families like mine in this emerging community of ethnic and racial diversity who were hardworking, home-owning, and churchgoing. But this family dynamic was not universal for the young people I grew up with. As the community became more under-resourced, I watched some struggling families fall apart. Now some of my friends had to navigate life without a father in the home. Some of them joined gangs.

Given the evacuation of businesses from our community, summer jobs were hard to find as I came of working age in my teens. I was fortunate that my grandmother owned a janitorial business. I didn't like cleaning toilets so much, but it was honest work, and she taught me the importance of earning money the right way. Every summer while I was in college, I took advantage of a local church's summer work program. But even as I worked, I watched others in my community sink further and further into a negative cash-flow system.

My community became more and more violent over time. By the time I was a young adult and married, my parents' house had been broken into, shot up, and set on fire. Even though my parents had insurance and the house was renovated, it wasn't the same to them, and they eventually moved to the suburbs.

Some look at the poor and explain their struggles solely in the context of a broken life. If those individual poor people would make an effort, the logic goes, they'd have a better life. We see America as this place where anyone who keeps their nose clean and does the right thing can make a good life. You could look at my life story and make a strong case for this position. But I know some that are working daily to do the right thing and are still trapped in a cycle of poverty. That's because poverty is not simply a matter of individual sin; it's also about broken relationships, broken systems, and broken institutions.

Under-resourced communities don't typically begin as under-resourced. The upside-down trinity of broken lives, broken relationships, and broken systems and structures conspire to kill communities. When businesses leave a community, that community struggles financially. It is also separated from the relational energy that comes with being connected to entrepreneurs. And unfortunately, in the United

States there has been a history of property values suffering when the number of white homeowners in a neighborhood goes down and the number of black and brown homeowners goes up. This is a combination of an unbiblical, racialized social system, and an economic system that perpetuates inequity. It's an upside-down world on a neighborhood scale.

Race is another example of the upside-downness of our world. There is no biological basis for "race." What we mean by race is not based on ethnicity or nationality; it has no correlation to particular behaviors or intelligences. It's based entirely on arbitrary classifications such as skin color. Furthermore, race is not a biblical concept: God did not create racial groups of human beings.

Nevertheless, race has been adopted as a social structure. It categorizes and places value on people based on physical features—the color of their skin, the shape of their nose, the size of their lips. Based on these attributes alone we make assumptions about who is fast, smart, and innovative and who has leadership potential. We also decide whom to fear, distrust, or even dislike.

Race is an obvious example of the world turned upside down. We ought to find our identity in God— we all were made in God's image. Yet I have lived my whole live in a social matrix that assumes I exhibit particular traits and embody particular values simply because I am black.

I am not ashamed of being black. But at the same time, I am more than black. I have ancestors who are Haitian, African, Native American, and Irish. I am truly a multiethnic human being. Most of us are, in fact. But I live in an upside-down world, which means I have to contend with the upside-down idea of race.

Consider some of the stereotypes of the black male: uneducated, a thug, a gangsta rapper, addicted to marijuana. Some broken people live into these caricatures of the black male; some broken people make millions of dollars off them.

Race impacts relationships through prejudice and racism, often culminating in violence. What would cause a white man in June 2015 to go into a black church in Charleston, South Carolina, and murder nine black people—after joining them for a Bible study? It takes an upside-down and broken life trapped in the sin of racism to do something so sinister. But even without this tragic example, far too many people allow the race matrix to fuel their everyday lives with ignorant assumptions about people of a different skin color.

And of course, race reaches all the way to our systems, structures, and institutions. In recent years we have seen an increase in tensions between police departments and under-resourced African American communities. Far too many unarmed African Americans have died in violent conflict with police officers. Some of those who died have engaged at some point in criminal behavior. But by no means have all of them done so, and there is evidence that many such deaths are connected to racial profiling within legal systems and institutions. Consider this: A white male goes into a movie theater with military weapons and kills a number of people. He is arrested. Another white male kills multiple people, including a police officer, and he is arrested. The white male who killed nine African Americans in a church is arrested. Meanwhile, multiple unarmed African Americans come up dead after their interactions with police. I am not painting all police officers as bad; I know many good police officers serving communities well, and we need a strong and productive police force in our society. But we must also admit that our systems, like our relationships and each of us as individuals, are broken and upside-down.

THE RIGHT-SIDE-UP REMNANT

So how are Christians to engage this upside-down world? Christ prays a prayer to his Father on behalf of his followers that is the beginning point for answering this question.

> I have given them your word, and the world
> has hated them because they are not of the
> world, just as I am not of the world. I do not

ask that you take them out of the world, but
that you keep them from the evil one. They are
not of the world, just as I am not of the world.
Sanctify them in the truth; your word is truth.
As you sent me into the world, so I have sent
them into the world.
John 17:14-18

As followers of Christ, we are to be in this upside-down world as a right-side-up remnant. We are to return to the work granted God's people when the world was right side up: to establish the Kingdom of God, where there is no brokenness, in our midst and to reproduce people who see the world right-side up. We do this by embracing a right-side-up life as beloved children of God, ambassadors of reconciliation, and citizens of the Kingdom of God.

Beloved Children of God

Through Christ Jesus we have become God's children—the well-loved of the heavenly Father.

See what kind of love the Father has given to
us, that we should be called children of God;
and so we are. The reason why the world
does not know us is that it did not know him.
Beloved, we are God's children now, and what
we will be has not yet appeared; but we know

that when he appears we shall be like him,
because we shall see him as he is.
1 John 3:1-2

As Christians we have had our identity flipped back right side up, having gone from being sinners separated from God to children in intimate relationship with the Father. The shed blood, death, and resurrection of Christ has repaired and restored us. We no longer have to seek identity and acceptance through performance or material things.

Living into this restored identity takes work, and it will look strange to people who have adjusted themselves to an upside-down world. Are you living as one dearly loved by God? As one who has been transformed by God's love and grace? Do you realize that there was nothing you did in your own power to receive this grace and love?

We help to turn the world right side up by embracing this identity for ourselves but also by embodying and extending God's love in our relationships. "Beloved, let us love one another, for love is from God, and whoever loves has been born of God and knows God" (1 John 4:7). As beloved children of God, we have access to God's love. If we are not living daily in God's extravagant love it is because we *choose* not to. This upside-down world, by contrast, is *not* a world of love. We occupy a world plagued with hate, prejudice, envy, individualism, selfishness, and jealousy. As a people of love, therefore, we are countercultural. Some will be threatened by us, because right-side-up love is incompatible with upside-down living.

Sometimes Christians come across as hateful, judgmental, individualistic, and prideful. We need to consider seriously and soberly whether this is because we are being perceived by an upside-down world or because we are giving in to upside-down values. God's credibility is not in question, but ours is. How will this upside-down world truly know that God is love if we don't live as the beloved? Broken people need to be impacted by beloved people.

Ambassadors of Reconciliation

In a world of broken relationships, there is a need for radical reconcilers. Christ is the great reconciler: Through his death and resurrection we have the opportunity to be brought back into right relationship with God. Now we who have been reconciled to God have been given the ministry of reconciliation in this upside-down world. "In Christ God was reconciling the world to himself, not counting their trespasses against them, and entrusting to us the message of reconciliation. Therefore we are ambassadors for Christ, God making his appeal through us" (2 Corinthians 5:19-20).

The Christian church comes across so divided

at times that we can be just as upside-down in our relationships as believers as this broken world. If we can't live in reconciling relationships with other Christians, how can we truly love our neighbors outside of the faith? How can we live into the biblical mandate to love our enemies?

We did nothing to deserve a reconciled and intimate relationship with God. With that awareness, and with Christ's selflessness as our model, we can enter into relationships with other people with humility about ourselves and gratitude and compassion toward them. Out of the overflow of God's love for us, we extend love to all people. This is what the right-side-up Kingdom God promises us will look like.

The family is the first place that Christians can model being ambassadors of reconciliation. We have an opportunity to show what right-side-up relationships look like right in our homes. How do you deal with conflict among family and friends? Do you extend grace, love, patience, and forgiveness? Are you the first to seek reconciliation in a broken relationship? These are the ways to live right side up in a world of upside-down relationships.

Citizens of the Kingdom of God

In a world of broken systems and institutions, the Christian has the opportunity to represent the eternal community of the Kingdom of God. We are citizens of a government born of our intimate relationship with God and our identity in Christ. However upside-down our citizenship in this Kingdom looks to our neighbors, we know by faith that it is God's vision for a world set right.

This eternal Kingdom is holistic—multiethnic, multicultural, multilingual, and Christ centered.

> After this I looked, and behold, a great multitude that no one could number, from every nation, from all tribes and peoples and languages, standing before the throne and before the Lamb, clothed in white robes, with palm branches in their hands, and crying out with a loud voice, "Salvation belongs to our God who sits on the throne, and to the Lamb!"
> *Revelation 7:9-10*

In the Kingdom of God there is no disease or poverty. Neither is there racism, or sexism, or oppression. There is peace and reconciliation in the eternal community of God. There is sustained praise and worship as well.

This is not just a community that we wait in anticipation of. We are to pray for the experience of this Kingdom right now.

Pray then like this:

Our Father in heaven,
hallowed be your name.
Your kingdom come,
your will be done,
    on earth as it is in heaven.
Matthew 6:9-10

This right-side-up Kingdom disrupts the upside-down systems and institutions in which we live daily, creating hunger in our hearts for something other-worldly to come. But is our purpose and mission just to pray for this to happen? No, we are to participate in the Kingdom of God coming to bear on this broken world.

When Jesus asks his disciples, "Who do people say that the Son of Man is?" Peter responds by saying, "You are the Christ, the Son of the living God." Christ makes the connections from there:

And I tell you, you are Peter, and on this rock I
will build my church, and the gates of hell shall
not prevail against it. I will give you the keys
of the kingdom of heaven, and whatever you
bind on earth shall be bound in heaven, and
whatever you loose on earth shall be loosed in
heaven.
Matthew 16:13-19

These are words of empowerment. We are children of God, citizens of the Kingdom of God, and empowered soldiers to advance this community of love, reconciliation, healing, and liberation in a world desperate for transformation.

They are also, however, words of war. Our citizenship in the Kingdom of God sets us against the kingdoms of this upside-down world. Our efforts at turning the world right-side up, of testifying to the right-side-upness of God, will be seen by some as threatening. When you've accepted a Bizarro world as normal life, the saving action of Christ can feel like a death. Even our own loyalties will be tested, as God's Kingdom touches on those areas of our life that we have not yet turned over to him. We will, every now and then, wonder why it seems that God is killing us.

But if God is killing us, he's doing so softly, tenderly, in order to raise us to new life. Instead of defending what is broken, we must lovingly and humbly embrace what is blessed and eternal.

As right-side-up people, we face a mission field, with a multitude of broken lives, broken relationships, and upside-down systems and institutions. The wonderful news is that the Son of God came into the upside-down world and gave his life so that broken lives could receive salvation and eternal life. Christ stepped into social structures of division between male and female, rich and poor, and Jew and Samaritan in order to present radical reconciliation. Christ declared and demonstrated the right-side-up Kingdom of God. As Christians we a have a missonal opportunity to live as witnesses to that Kingdom until such time as Christ returns—to provide a sneak preview of the world set right.

FOR REFLECTION AND DISCUSSION

What in your context suggests that we live in an upside-down world?

How have you experienced God setting your life right side up?

What gives you hope that the Kingdom of God can transform the upside-down lives and systems around you?

3

JESUS: THE RIGHT-SIDE-UP WAY, TRUTH, AND LIFE

A FEW YEARS AGO the CBS television network launched a reality television show called *Undercover Boss*. There are versions of this reality show in various countries around the world today. The concept centers around a senior executive or owner of a company who goes undercover to find out what is really going on in his or her business. Taking on the identity of an entry-level employee, these executives go from their office suites to the factory floor, the kitchen, the cash register, or the service garage. They experience firsthand the messy details of the day-to-day operations of the business. As a result, they discover things that need to be addressed to make their businesses better.

At the end of the show the senior executive reveals

his or her true identity to the employees they have been working beside the whole time. An employee who has been doing a good job is congratulated and rewarded. An employee who has compromised the business is reprimanded, even punished.

We shouldn't make a direct comparison of these undercover bosses to God's only begotten Son. But there are some general similarities. Thinking of Jesus' mission in a similar way can lead to a fuller appreciation of God's ministry to this upside-down world.

When Christ came into this world, God became one of us. He took on the form of man. As he declared and demonstrated what the world could look like, he invited people into the right-side-up life, which he called the Kingdom of God.

God didn't need to enter this world in order to discover what the challenges were, of course. God knew that humanity was enslaved to sin. God knew that humankind had rebelled against his original plan for them. God knew that broken people and systems were killing his creation. God entered the world not to find out whether it was broken but to set things right again.

This is what makes John 3:16 so powerful. God sent his Son into the world not because of self-interest, like a business owner checking on the integrity of the business, but because of love—the unconditional and undeniable, radical and revolutionary love of God.

In the Old Testament we find God's love mentioned

many times. God's people celebrate that his "steadfast love and . . . faithfulness will ever preserve me!" (Psalm 40:11). Elsewhere they appeal to God to "redeem us for the sake of your steadfast love" (Psalm 44:26). The prophet Isaiah anticipates "one who judges and seeks justice and is swift to do righteousness" from a throne that is "established in steadfast love" (Isaiah 16:5). The prophet Hosea assures us that in love God will "betroth you to [himself] forever . . . in righteousness and in justice, in steadfast love and in mercy" (Hosea 2:19). The prophet Micah assures us that God "does not retain his anger forever, because he delights in steadfast love" (Micah 7:18). Love is God's primary motivator.

In the upside-down world in which we live, other motivations drive people into spaces, positions, and relationships. Sometimes we befriend people at work because we hope they will help us get promoted. Some people seek to enter into a new position for the power and prestige it will afford them. Some people seek to enter into a certain community primarily because it represents how successful they have become. It is becoming more and more rare in this upside-down world to find people entering into certain positions and sectors out of the primary motivation of love and service.

Consider politics, for instance. It's becoming more and more difficult to seek political offices—whether mayor, governor, or president—with the primary motivation being service and love of people. Our upside-down reality has created a climate where power, ego, celebrity, and narcissism are expected and acceptable motivations for public service. Similarly, in the private sector the motivation of success has led some CEOs to have a "win at all costs" attitude. Even in the church, the upside-down world has found influence. In some cases it is not enough to seek the calling of pastor based on a primary motivation of love for people and a specific community. There are pastors who are motivated to be the next celebrity pastor, church-growth guru, or business CEO.

The good news is that even in the midst of those upside-down realities, there are some right-side-up examples of people who are motivated enough by the possibility of transformation to be willing to look strange. Consider Pat, who is the CEO of VMWare, a successful company in Silicon Valley in Northern California. He is motivated by something much deeper than just how much profit his company brings in annually. He considers himself a pastor to the people of his company. That doesn't mean Pat is preaching to his employees. Rather, he roots his work in the motivation of love that God has placed within him. He has a heart for the people who work for him. He also has a heart for the Bay Area of Northern California. Because of this, he used his influence to assist in starting the organization Transforming the Bay with Christ (TBC). He desires to see the love of God transform the Bay Area, one of the most unchurched metropolitan areas in the nation, through church planting, collaborative church service projects, and an evangelism strategy contextualized for that specific mission field. Meeting Pat has given me an example of what a right-side-up businessperson can look like.

In the political realm, I think of a man named Don. He has been involved in local politics in Minneapolis for a number of years. He is motivated by a love for the urban community and its children and families. Don served on the city council representing one of the most under-resourced communities of Minneapolis. He was passionate about bringing attention to the community and reducing violence there. Whenever someone died violently in the community, he would hold a prayer vigil at the spot where the murder occurred. He would spend a whole day at that spot instead of being at his office. There were probably times when he missed a city-council meeting because he was sitting on a street corner looking down at the dried blood of a young person who died senselessly and too soon. Don eventually ran for mayor of Minneapolis. He didn't win, but this didn't quench his motivation. His heart for the community and service led him next to run successfully for the school board. He is now inside the upside-down system of urban public education, advocating for urban youth and families.

In the area of ministry, there is Amy. A veteran

urban-youth worker, Amy is a gifted preacher and youth ministry trainer. She could pursue success by seeking to become the next celebrity evangelist. Instead, she lives in a very challenging community in Chicago and calls herself a "hope dealer." She has become a big sister and auntie to many at-risk and high-risk youth. She visits young people who are incarcerated, extending God's love to them even when their behavior has led others to distance themselves from them. She uses her platform to call the church to lament when the lives of urban young people are cut short by violence. I can't imagine the burden she must carry in her heart as she puts her own life in danger at times to bring hope, grace, and transformation to young lives.

Of course I will come across as biased, but I am surrounded by an army of right-side-up people at World Impact, an urban Christian missions organization where I serve as president and CEO. One example of this is Pastor Curtis Flemming, our Bay Area director and senior pastor of Bay Community Fellowship in Oakland. He has served as a pastor and district superintendent for his denomination in New York City. There have been many opportunities for denominational leadership that he could have pursued (and there would have been nothing wrong with that). Instead, a few years ago, God led him and his wife, Nancy, along with their sons, to West Oakland. Within the World Impact facility, he planted Bay Community Fellowship.

Out of this small community church has come a day-care center, a discipleship home for men coming out of prison who have given their lives to Christ and desire to become ministry leaders, and an outreach to children (the church adopted a nearby elementary school).

These are just a few examples of how God's love is causing his beloved children to enter into sectors of this upside-down world for transformation. Being willing to allow God to kill us softly for a purpose is about being open to alterations in our life plans. It may mean moving away from a life plan that seems right in this world. It could mean sacrificing privilege or a powerful position for an opportunity that might seem strange to others. When we follow God in these countercultural ways, we discover more deeply the lengths to which God went in order to make life transformation possible for us. God was willing to get low and dwell in this upside-down world so that we could experience new life, liberating love, and deliverance from the death sentence of sin.

Jesus announced his ministry to the world by reading from the prophet Isaiah:

> He unrolled the scroll and found the place
> where it was written,
>
> "The Spirit of the Lord is upon me,
>   because he has anointed me
>   to proclaim good news to the poor.

He has sent me to proclaim liberty to the captives
   and recovering of sight to the blind,
   to set at liberty those who are oppressed,
to proclaim the year of the Lord's favor."

And he rolled up the scroll and gave it back to
the attendant and sat down. And the eyes of all
in the synagogue were fixed on him. And he
began to say to them, "Today this Scripture has
been fulfilled in your hearing."
Luke 4:17-21

The text makes clear, and Jesus' pronouncement con-
firms, that God is not satisfied with the world remain-
ing upside-down. God is interested in the deliverance,
liberation, empowerment, and transformation of
upside-down people and in the introduction of an
alternative to an upside-down world.

Jesus didn't just declare this profound message; he
demonstrated it, showing the countercultural character of God's Kingdom and showing himself to be the
way, the truth, and the right-side-up life.

ENTRY LEVEL

Christ came into the world at the entry level of humanity. He came in the human package of the poor, the
marginalized, and the multiethnic. Once he arrived,

Christ sought fellowship, community, and solidarity with other human beings in the low places of society. A broken world could identify with Christ because he bore the marks of brokenness.

After Jesus read from Isaiah's scroll, "all spoke well of him and marveled at the gracious words that were coming from his mouth. And they said, 'Is not this Joseph's son?'" (Luke 4:22). They were struck that someone so like them was bringing a message so profound. But they quickly turned on him when he pointed out that his message was contrary to the way they had grown accustomed to living.

> When they heard these things, all in the
> synagogue were filled with wrath. And they
> rose up and drove him out of the town and
> brought him to the brow of the hill on which
> their town was built, so that they could throw
> him down the cliff.
> *Luke 4:28-29*

In today's world of terrorism, racial tensions, immigration debates, the need for criminal justice reform, and a widening gap between the haves and the have-nots, the hardship Christ entered into is worth observing. Even his upbringing would put into question his claims to a kingdom. A question hovered over the value of his hometown: "Can anything good come out of Nazareth?" (John 1:46). His earthly father was not a king but a common carpenter, a blue-collar worker. His people were subjects of the oppressive Roman Empire. He was quickly subjected to a kind of "racial profiling" that forced his family to become refugees: Under the instruction of the governing authority, every male baby who looked like Jesus was murdered (Matthew 2:16-18).

Christ came in the human package of the vulnerable and despised so that he would have a deep and intimate credibility with the most marginalized and oppressed around him—the diseased, the outcast, the left-for-dead, the demonized, and the poverty-stricken. Jesus' life was as radical and relevant as his message way back then. It remains so today.

JESUS' FAMILY TREE

We continue, for the most part, to portray Christ as white, European, and pure and clean and well-dressed. This version of Christ is not only unbiblical, it limits our evangelism, discipleship, and Kingdom advancement.

According to Jesus' genealogy found in Matthew 1, Jesus was multiethnic, with Hebrew, African, and Asiatic ancestors. According to Genesis 12, Abraham, mentioned early on in Jesus' genealogy, was born in Ur—modern-day Iraq. Tamar, mentioned in Matthew 1:3, was a descendant of Canaan (see Genesis 38), the grandson of Noah, whom Noah cursed because Canaan's father Ham failed to cover up Noah when he was in a drunken and naked state (see Genesis 9:18-27). Because of her Canaanite heritage, Tamar would have been seen by Jesus' own community as cursed. Moreover, based on the story of her life told in Genesis 38, she was surrounded by scandal.

If Jesus were walking in physical form in the United States today, he would be considered an ethnic minority, a person of color. He very well might be pulled over by the police for driving around the wrong neighborhood after dark. He might be followed around the shopping mall by security.

There is more to uncover in the family tree of Christ. The Canaanites were the original inhabitants of the places we call Egypt, Ethiopia, Sudan, Libya, Israel, and Palestine today. This means that Egyptians, Ethiopians, Sudanese, Libyans, Israelis, and Palestinians are all in the bloodline of Jesus as the Son of Man. Some of these nations were enemies of Israel; other ancestors of Jesus were tainted by scandal. Within his bloodline are the oppressed, the oppressor, the cursed, the poor, the wealthy, and the marginalized. The full diversity and brokenness of humanity flowed through his veins.

So to portray Christ as white, European, wealthy, glamorously handsome, and from the "right side of the tracks" is to turn Christ upside down. Presumably this has been done mainly for the comfort and uplifting of a dominant racial group.

A white Jesus unfortunately hints at a history of colonization, American slavery, and a religious culture that reinforces a privileged class. The fact that the majority of churches in the United States are still racially segregated may be rooted in the continued neglect of Jesus' multiethnic heritage and his non-European background.

Even saying that causes some people alarm. I have communicated with some Christian leaders who seem willing to fight for the defense of a false representation of Jesus. Others just seem apathetic to the whole discussion. It seems that for a great number of Christians, a color-blind approach to Jesus is the best route. But color blindness regarding Jesus doesn't neutralize the question. It actually reinforces the dominant, inaccurate portrayal of Jesus and the upside-down systems that such a false representation has made possible.

Not too long ago, my youngest daughter asked me whether I was trying to make Jesus black because I'm black. White Jesus, she told me, is the only Jesus she has ever known; it would be challenging for her to see Jesus any other way.

I told my family that evening that it was not my intention to make Jesus black. But neither should we make Jesus white. The authentic Jesus of the Scriptures was neither white nor black but multiethnic. This multiethnicity is important: Even in his body, Christ is the great reconciler, doing the hard work of bringing people together and setting things and people right side up.

The real Jesus forces the church to become a suffering, reconciling, liberating, and transforming movement all at the same time. Maybe this is why we want the false Jesus. It's so much easier to live in comfort.

THE MINISTRY OF JESUS

Knowing and following the authentic Christ is about more than understanding his multicultural and multi-ethnic identity when he walked the earth. As an adult, Christ formally launched his "campaign for King." His strange words and actions in this campaign are the very key to making things right in this upside-down world.

In his interactions with people, Jesus both declared and demonstrated the Kingdom of God. He gave sight to the blind. He gave mobility to the paralyzed. He allowed a diseased and outcast woman to touch him and find healing. He raised people from the dead. He delivered people from the evil spirits that terrorized them from the inside. He shared meals with tax collectors and other sinners. He stood between stones and a woman caught in adultery. In all these things, he demonstrated the actions of a life set straight, a world founded on God's love and grace.

In his teaching, Jesus speaks on living life right side up. In contrast to the priorities of this world—consumption, individualism, materialism, power at the expense of others, division, and violence as the primary means for solving conflict—Jesus "blesses" people who are meek, peacemakers, pure in heart, willing to be persecuted for righteousness. He calls these people the salt of the earth and the light of the world (Matthew 5). Could it be that Christ was presenting a way of living that pointed back to God's initial idea for humanity? These blessings evoke a world of stewardship, cooperation, unity, and fruitfulness.

Christ's teaching is not simplistic. He identifies the connections between personal sin, relational sin, and sinful systems and structures.

> You have heard that it was said to those of old, "You shall not murder; and whoever murders will be liable to judgment." But I say to you that anyone who is angry with his brother will be liable to judgment. . . .
> You have heard that it was said, "You shall not commit adultery." But I say to you that everyone who looks at a woman with lustful intent has already committed adultery with her in his heart.
> *Matthew 5:21-28*

The upside-down world begins with broken lives, and broken lives begin with broken hearts. Sin enters the innermost part of a person and turns their life upside down.

Right-side-up living begins by recognizing that my heart isn't right apart from God. I can't repair it in my own power. I need the love of God shown through Jesus Christ to mend my broken heart. I must repent of my sins: the outward behavior stemming from my upside-down life and broken heart.

As I follow Christ and grow as a disciple, I extend God's love by loving my neighbor as myself. Christ acknowledges this as the second great commandment of Scripture (Matthew 22:36-40). He also contrasts the command against the upside-down practices of the day—even by people characterized as religious authorities. He confronts people who are preoccupied by what they "give God" in their offerings, while neglecting people in need:

Woe to you, scribes and Pharisees, hypocrites! For you tithe mint and dill and cumin, and have neglected the weightier matters of the law: justice and mercy and faithfulness. These you ought to have done, without neglecting the others. You blind guides, straining out a gnat and swallowing a camel!
Matthew 23:23-24

He points out the inevitable hypocrisy in this upside-down religion, as religious people break one of the Ten Commandments in order to curry favor with God:

> God commanded, "Honor your father and your mother," and, "Whoever reviles father or mother must surely die." But you say, "If anyone tells his father or his mother, 'What you would have gained from me is given to God,' he need not honor his father." So for the sake of your tradition you have made void the word of God. You hypocrites! Well did Isaiah prophesy of you, when he said:
>
> "This people honors me with their lips,
>   but their heart is far from me;
> in vain do they worship me,
>   teaching as doctrines the commandments
>   of men."
> *Matthew 15:4-9*

It is possible to be a Christian and still on some level behave as an arrogant, selfish, unforgiving, and prejudiced person. This behavior does not mean that my heart has not been changed, that I have not been made holy and righteous by God. It is a reminder rather that we live the right-sided life *by faith*. We must come before God daily with our faults and behavior that point us back to the upside-down life. This world is killing us; God is doing the same, but the death he brings us through is in service to the new life he has for us: "If anyone would come after me, let him deny himself and take up his cross and follow me. For whoever would save his life will lose it, but whoever loses his life for my sake will find it" (Matthew 16:24-25).

This is why an intimate relationship with God, experiencing God's love and grace daily, is important. We must live in God's love in order to be people who love God and love our neighbor as ourselves.

In case we were starting to feel comfortable with loving our neighbor, Christ goes on to further complicate it:

> You have heard that it was said, "You shall love your neighbor and hate your enemy." But I say to you, Love your enemies and pray for those who persecute you, so that you may be sons of your Father who is in heaven.
> *Matthew 5:43-45*

The right-side-up life is so transformed by God's love that there is love in the heart even for enemies and those who seek to do us harm. This is a crazy love indeed. But this kind of love can bring about transformation in an upside-down world.

We saw this kind of love during the Civil Rights

Movement. Dr. Martin Luther King Jr. should not just be known for leading a church-based and nonviolent movement for justice and equality. What set him apart as a right-side-up leader was his unique message of loving your enemy. In his context, the enemy was racist white people and the systems of white supremacy that they had built and defended. King believed that the love of God shown through Christ Jesus was powerful enough to change the hearts even of oppressors. Some question whether this strategy was successful. I believe that it was and that it still is. Kingdom justice comes about through a radical reconciliation driven by revolutionary love.

Christ would show us the ultimate act of God's love for us. He would live out sacrificial love by dying on the cross. This again is a strange way for someone to become a king. Instead of inflicting violence upon others in order to seize power, Christ endured suffering, affliction, violence, and death. He experienced incarceration, brutality, and capital punishment in order to make the way for people to be set right. He ascended to his throne after first being embarrassed, ridiculed, and shamed. Who would follow a king like this?

This is where the tension arrived for the first followers of Christ. When Christ was healing, giving sight to the blind, and feeding thousands, his followership grew and grew. When he was arrested and prepared for crucifixion, many abandoned him; one of his closest followers denied ever knowing him.

It is worth pointing out that Jesus' actions and teachings would be attractive to people seeking revolution. Many of Christ's first followers were people eager to participate in a revolt against the Roman Empire. Some were Zealots—rebels who were waiting for someone to lead a violent resistance movement. What other strategy would there be for overturning an oppressive government in an upside down world?

The authorities certainly saw Jesus as a threat to their power, an enemy to be dispensed with; that's what got him arrested. And some of his actions were certainly provocative, the most obvious example being his cleansing of the Temple:

> In the temple he found those who were selling oxen and sheep and pigeons, and the money-changers sitting there. And making a whip of cords, he drove them all out of the temple, with the sheep and oxen. And he poured out the coins of the money-changers and overturned their tables. And he told those who sold the pigeons, "Take these things away; do not make my Father's house a house of trade." His disciples remembered that it was written, "Zeal for your house will consume me."
>
> So the Jews said to him, "What sign do you show us for doing these things?" Jesus answered them, "Destroy this temple, and in

three days I will raise it up." The Jews then said,
"It has taken forty-six years to build this temple,
and will you raise it up in three days?" But he
was speaking about the temple of his body.
John 2:14-21

Here we see Jesus confronting a system, established to serve the religious life of his community,
that had been corrupted by the brokenness that characterizes an upside-down world. Broken people, broken relationships, and broken systems—all these were
on Jesus' agenda for transformation. No wonder the
revolutionaries loved him.

But the revolution Christ led was not what the
upside-down people around him expected. His strategy was not one of violence but of love, his revolution rooted in the heart, his Kingdom not temporal but
eternal. This countercultural gospel led Christ to the
cross—a strategy the apostle Paul encourages Christ's
followers to emulate:

Have this mind among yourselves, which is
yours in Christ Jesus, who, though he was
in the form of God, did not count equality
with God a thing to be grasped, but emptied
himself, by taking the form of a servant,
being born in the likeness of men. And being
found in human form, he humbled himself by

becoming obedient to the point of death, even
death on a cross.
Philippians 2:5-8

Because of sin, this world and human lives are
turned upside down. But God's mysterious grace and
steadfast love won't allow it to stay that way. God sent
his only Son into the world in order to set things right.
God showed up in this upside-down world, becoming
like us but pointing us and leading us to a world that
is right side up. Ultimately Christ and the Kingdom of
God are not upside-down; they appear to be upside-
down only because *we* actually are. If we are going to
truly live as right-side-up people, we must join Christ,
which involves dying to our upside-down selves.
This isn't an easy journey—death never is—but when
empowered by God, our lives can provide a glimpse
of what the eternal right-sided community looks like.

QUESTIONS FOR REFLECTION AND DISCUSSION

How has the right-side-up Kingdom of God been
showing up in your life lately?

What are the areas in your life where God can
continue the work of turning you right side up?

How can you be God's vehicle of entering into
an upside-down world for transformation?

4

TO FOLLOW CHRIST YOU HAVE TO DIE

THE SOULFUL SINGER Roberta Flack sings a song about a woman in a nightclub. Her heart is heavy and sad. She sits at the bar, probably with a drink in her hand, while a man on stage is performing. We're told that *she* is there because *he* is there: "I heard he sang a good song; I heard he had a style . . ."

As the song progresses, we get the impression that the experience is not what she expected. The song the man is singing has a powerful impact on the woman. It's as if he knows her whole life story. She feels exposed by his performance—he is, she sings, "killing me softly with his song."

As uncomfortable as the scene sounds, there is something soothing to this song. It's like the story of Christ sitting at a well with a Samaritan woman (John 4).

Jesus has found himself in Samaria, a community that is considered off-limits to Jewish people. Jesus' peers in Jerusalem and the surrounding communities saw Samaritans as subhuman. So it's odd to begin with that Jesus is there.

A nameless Samaritan woman comes to the well where Jesus is resting. She's there to get water. Christ asks her for a drink. She is taken aback that this Jewish man would talk to her. As they talk, he reveals that he knows her somewhat scandalous story: She has been married multiple times; she is currently living with a man who is not her husband. How can this strange Jewish man know this?

In another story from the Gospels, a woman found to be in a similar circumstance is brought to Jesus to be stoned to death (John 8). That was how the upside-down world dealt with broken people. Specifically, we see throughout the Scriptures how an upside-down world treats women, especially marginalized and out-cast women. When Christ encounters broken people, however, he chooses a different way.

What we see Jesus doing with the Samaritan woman at the well might be called "soul surgery." He is undoing her story: telling her whole life with his words, bringing up the things that are uncomfortable. He's killing her softly. But that's not where he leaves things: By killing her softly in this way, Jesus is preparing her to be born again.

At the end of their conversation, the woman gets up from the well and tells everyone about the man whom she now knows as the Christ. She has experienced reconciliation—not just between a Jew and a Samaritan, between a man and a woman, but also between a broken person and a holy God. She has also embraced a mission: She is now a follower of Christ, an agent of reconciliation in the world.

This in itself is revolutionary. Women in Jesus' day were not empowered to exert influence on culture. The role of a woman in the social structure of a broken world was subservient. Yet here she was, being transformed in every way by the Son of God.

This is what life with God can look like. Christ meets us in unexpected places, brings up uncomfortable issues, turns us right side up, and awakens us to our true purpose. All of us can experience this transformative process, being killed softly and lovingly by God, being resurrected in his image and for his glory.

Dying daily is not comfortable, of course, but it's necessary for growing and maturing as a Christian. I have to be willing to allow God to reveal those things that still linger within my being that must be given over to the dying process, those things that I have not fully turned over to Christ so he can turn them right side up in my life. I must allow God to kill me softly with his love and grace.

This approach to Christian formation embraces the reality that we are works in process. We are not yet as we will be, but we are on the way. We shouldn't live in guilt and shame over the places where we still are falling short. Instead, in God's love, we can press on toward who we ought to be in him.

God will not leave us to do this work alone. Maybe this is why Christ invites us to come to him?

Come to me, all who labor and are heavy laden, and I will give you rest. Take my yoke upon you, and learn from me, for I am gentle and lowly in heart, and you will find rest for your souls. For my yoke is easy, and my burden is light.
Matthew 11:28-30

HOW I WOULD LIKE TO DIE

Some of us have watched loved ones die in ways that are painful to our hearts. Maybe these experiences and thoughts on natural death cause us to shy away from the spiritual death process. Not that there is no discomfort from the spiritual dying process, but there is a rest as well. Dying in Christ is an opportunity to dance with our Creator. It is an opportunity to be comforted, healed, strengthened, and empowered. It is an opportunity to experience the presence of the Holy Spirit at the deepest place of who we truly are.

My father loves the blues. B. B. King, Bobby Blue Bland, and Johnny Taylor are artists I grew up hearing as a child because of my father. He would play records by these artists on the stereo in our house most weekends. There was one song he played that I still remember today, even though I can't remember who the artist was who sang it. The chorus of the song states, "Everybody wants to go to heaven, but nobody wants to die."

For me, that lyric was both true and haunting. And if I'm honest, I still carry some concern about dying. I have a passion for advancing God's Kingdom in the here and now, and I have an exciting anticipation of one day being in paradise with my Creator. But it's that moving from this life into the next that can still be a struggle for me.

Now, if God would ask me, I would tell God how I would like to die:

On my hundredth birthday, I want to wake up at about noon.

I want to have a meal that consists of collard greens, macaroni and cheese, fried catfish, and corn bread.

I want to wash that meal down with some grape soda.

Following that meal, I want a bowl of warm peach cobbler with three scoops of vanilla bean ice cream.

After that, I want to fall into a peaceful sleep.

When I open my eyes, I want to be in heaven.

This is how I want to die. I don't want my death to be violent. I don't want to suffer with a disease. I want to have that down-home Southern and African American cultural meal at midday, and then I want to transition to that sweet by-and-by. This is my vision for my death.

Here's the problem: God has not asked me how I want to die. I don't fully control how I will die. Even if I work out four times a week, eat healthy, take my vitamins daily, and get eight hours of sleep every night, my life is in God's hands. I am vulnerable to this broken, upside-down, and sinful world.

The vulnerability of our ultimate, final, physical death is comparable to what God invites us into daily: a spiritual death characterized by vulnerability. Paul speaks to the spiritual dying process in the book of Galatians:

> I have been crucified with Christ. It is no longer I who live, but Christ who lives in me. And the life I now live in the flesh I live by faith in the Son of God, who loved me and gave himself for me. I do not nullify the grace of God, for if righteousness were through the law, then Christ died for no purpose.
> *Galatians 2:20-21*

Dying to live is a framework for our Christian formation. It is easy and appropriate to praise God for the resurrection of Christ and the new life he offers us. But how can we truly live as resurrected beings if we haven't first embraced our death in Christ? The beginning of Christ's victory over death is Christ taking on death.

Death for the Christian is a temporary experience on the way to an eternally right-side-up community. The more I die to the upside-down life, the more I experience life as the right-side-up, beloved child of God. The more I'm willing to die, the more I can experience new life as a citizen of the Kingdom of God.

What does dying daily look like? Paul helps us once again.

> So if there is any encouragement in Christ,
> any comfort from love, any participation in the
> Spirit, any affection and sympathy, complete my
> joy by being of the same mind, having the same
> love, being in full accord and of one mind. Do
> nothing from selfish ambition or conceit, but
> in humility count others more significant than
> yourselves. Let each of you not only look to his
> own interests, but also to the interests of others.
> *Philippians 2:1-4*

Paul may have been referring to the people going deeper in their experience of Christ individually and collectively so that he would know that his own labor and suffering was worth it. Possibly Paul was thinking that he could now face his own physical death knowing that there was a radical community of believers in Christ dying daily in order to truly live and lead more people to their own spiritual deaths and rebirths in Christ. Ultimately, Paul was inviting the Philippian Christians to consider the things to which they needed to die in their minds, hearts, and wills in order to live more completely and consistently as the community of Christ in troubled times. We must consider dying daily in these same areas today.

THE MIND SET RIGHT

What are the things we need to die to in our thinking? Are there belief systems that block our ability to meditate on the things of God? A significant part of living the transformed life of a Christ follower is a renewed mind. "Do not be conformed to this world, but be transformed by the renewal of your mind, that by testing you may discern what is the will of God, what is good and acceptable and perfect" (Romans 12:2).

Our minds are full of things that remain upsidedown to the Kingdom of God. We have worldly beliefs about ourselves, others, and the world in which we live. Some people are trapped into thinking that they will never amount to anything. Some people are trapped by superstitious ideas. Some people are held captive by hurtful and abusive words spoken by a person who they believed loved them. That playground saying, "Sticks and stones may break my bones, but words will never hurt me" is not true. Words do hurt. Word can enslave a person and cause them to live below God's purpose for their lives.

Paul understood the power of words over a young person's life. We see an example of this as Paul encourages young Timothy:

> Let no one despise you for your youth, but set the believers an example in speech, in conduct, in love, in faith, in purity. Until I come, devote yourself to the public reading of Scripture, to exhortation, to teaching. Do not neglect the gift you have, which was given you by prophecy when the council of elders laid their hands on you.
> *1 Timothy 4:12-14*

Timothy knew he was gifted; the elders of the church had laid hands over him and spoken into his life. He would have been encouraged and empowered by Paul's words here. But if it's true that words can give you the right mindset about who you are in Christ, then it's also true that words can be destructive and create a deceptive mindset. Are there false thoughts, corrupted beliefs, and abusive words swirling around your mind? Lift them up to the Lord daily. Confess these bad beliefs representing the upside-down world. Die to them daily until such time as they have no life in your thinking.

Another way of dying to things that aren't of God in our minds is to meditate daily on the truth of who we are in God. Through prayer, Bible study, and journaling we can experience the renewing of our minds. We need to remind ourselves on a daily basis that we are beloved children of God, that we are precious jewels, that we are valuable, and that God has given us resources to accomplish his purposes in our lives. These positive, biblical messages do battle with the negative messages that come at us from the broken individuals and systems that surround us. They help us die to the world and live into the Kingdom.

Our right-side-up minds are not for our own edification alone. We can also have a transformative impact on others in their thinking. We can become agents of God's work in the world by encouraging others toward the renewing of their minds. When my two daughters were little girls, they would ask me questions such as "Am I beautiful?" I wondered whether they asked these types of questions because the upside-down world was already leading them, at such an early age, to believe they were "less than." When they would sometimes ask me questions about their skin color, I would wonder whether they had been given a message that black and brown skin isn't beautiful, or not as beautiful as white skin. I decided that my words could help to kill anything in their minds that would cause them to think less of themselves than they should. So when I would tuck them into bed at night, I would pray for them, kiss them, and then tell them to repeat after me: "I am beautiful. I am a queen. I am a champion. I am God's daughter."

My daughters, Jaeda and Mireya, are now twenty and seventeen years old. Jaeda recently told me that her belief in her beauty and giftedness is based on those words that I spoke over her when she was a little girl. I had almost forgotten about those days of tucking her and Mireya in bed at night. All these years later, they had not forgotten.

At World Impact, we have an initiative called The Urban Ministry Institute (TUMI). It's seminary-level theological education and leadership development for the urban poor, the incarcerated, and under-resourced urban ministry leaders. Students participate in a sixteen-module program and graduate with a certificate in urban ministry leadership. TUMI was developed by Dr. Don Davis, an African American whose journey took him from a life dealing drugs on the streets of inner-city Wichita, Kansas, to earning a PhD from the Iowa School of Religion in theology and ethics. His once upside-down life was set right side up through the transforming power of Christ.

TUMI is based on a satellite model of education and leadership development. There are over 240 satellites in cities around the country, in prisons and county jails, and—partnering with indigenous ministries—in multiple countries around the world. It is a movement of God killing people softly within their minds and then resurrecting them into a Kingdom mindset. Why would I state that? Because the curriculum that makes up TUMI is rooted in the idea that the poor, marginalized, and incarcerated have just as much right to participate in the great commission as anyone else. There are students who are incarcerated and have become Christians who are learning for the first time that not only can they receive salvation in Christ Jesus, but they also are invited to join Christ in his mission in the world. For many of these incarcerated students this is a revolutionary thought: Regardless of the circumstances that led to their present situation, they are valuable to God. They are no longer drug dealers, gang members, abusers, or thieves. They are now disciple-makers, being used by God in church-planting movements and revival, in local communities after their release, or in prison communities for the duration of their sentence.

Out of two hundred-plus men released from prisons and county jails who have participated in TUMI, only 6 percent have gone back to prison. Out of that 6 percent, only one person went to jail for a new offense; the others went back because of parole violations.

I have visited some of the inmates who are participating in TUMI. I tell them that if they are going to be released soon, they can go into the world with the mind-set that God has killed and is killing their old person; they are no longer convicts but are now called ones, invited to new lives as vehicles of God's love, truth, and reconciliation in the world. There are a number of testimonies of what God is doing through TUMI, especially among the formerly incarcerated. One young man, a recent TUMI graduate, has been released from prison and is currently planting a church. Another young man who participated in TUMI while incarcerated is now out of prison, employed, and interning at an urban church. He, too, hopes to one day plant a church.

Powerful things can happen when the mind is renewed. But it's not just the poor, incarcerated, and marginalized who need to experience dying to self in the area of bad thinking. There are people of privilege and great influence who also need God to kill some of the things that they think about themselves, other people, and the world around them. As a former church planter, missions organization leader, and teaching pastor in an urban and multiethnic church, I continue to have concern over how divided the church is in the United States. Still one of the most racially segregated institutions in the nation, the church is also segregated by political persuasion and even socioeconomic class.

It causes me to wonder whether our mind-sets are more dominated by this upside-down world than we would like to admit. Are we held more captive to political ideologies than we are to Kingdom values? Are we worshiping our own knowledge and education over the revelation, wisdom, and insights of God? This is not to take away from the importance of education, but we can become idolatrous of our own minds, believing that our rational reasoning is superior to what we find in the Bible. We must align our minds with the truth of God's Word and the truth of who we are in Christ in order to live right side up in this upside-down world.

THE HEART SET RIGHT

Just because our minds are being renewed as God kills the things in our thinking that hold us captive to this upside-down world, that doesn't mean we are fully aligned with God's purpose for our lives. We must also die to things that are not of God in our hearts.

There are things of this world that hold our hearts captive. There are feelings that are real and contaminate our hearts. These feelings should not be denied, because they are there, but they *can* be replaced as we grow deeper in our intimate relationship with God.

We die to feelings of abandonment as we live into our adoption by God.

We die to feelings of rejection from someone we

thought loved us as we live into the reality of being dearly loved by a God who will never forsake us.

The greatest strength of King Solomon in the Old Testament was his wisdom—wisdom he requested and received from God (1 Kings 3:5-15). This wisdom allowed him to settle disputes, acquire wealth, and build God's Temple. But even with all this wisdom, Solomon would set the stage for the kingdom of Israel to be divided through his heart problem. Though wise, Solomon took multiple women as wives and concubines. Many of these women worshiped foreign gods, and his relationships with them led him to commit idolatry with their gods. Solomon's seven hundred wives and three hundred concubines turned his heart away from the true God, who had given him not only wisdom but riches and honor as well. Though he was wise in his mind, Solomon's heart was not fully committed to God (1 Kings 11:1-8).

Solomon's heart problem led to a whole nation becoming divided. Recall the connection between individual sin and broken systems. It is possible to be a godly person and yet, because of a heart problem, to divide families, communities, and even whole people groups. This is a major reason why we see very smart leaders in politics, business, entertainment, and religion fall because of scandals. There are politicians who wisely navigate a challenging economy, for example, but who are forced to step out of politics because of an affair. There are pastors who have the wisdom to grow large churches, but their damaged hearts cause them to abuse staff. There are business leaders who are able to successfully lead multiple businesses but show signs of great immaturity in their relationships with people. An upside-down heart contaminated by jealousy, pride, arrogance, and lust can kill a marriage and even a church.

I have sat in church meetings with very smart people whose hearts weren't right. I must admit that there have been moments when I've been the one in the church meeting whose heart wasn't right. You can be a very wise Christian and do damage to your household, business, church, or community because you refuse to acknowledge the things in your heart that need to die. We must be willing to allow God to do soul surgery on us.

Heart issues within adults that point back to damage done to them as children can contaminate their relations with their own children, damaging another generation of hearts. When I was a youth pastor, I remember meeting a young man who was very wise for his age. We could talk about sports, politics, music, or race. This teenager had so much potential. But his heart was damaged. When we first started meeting in the church youth center, he had already dropped out of high school. He was involved in a gang and was selling drugs. He told me that before he dropped out he was getting all As and Bs in his classes. Why would someone so head-smart drop out of school and become a teenage drug dealer?

As he shared his story with me, it became clear that he hadn't joined the gang simply to make fast money. He had been born into a gang family. His mother both sold and used drugs, and she had forced him to sell drugs on the street when he was in elementary school. When he would go to school instead of selling drugs on the corner for her, she would beat him with a broom or baseball bat. He would still sneak to school as much as he could, and he was able to get through his sopho-more year in high school. But word would get back to his mother, and he would take another beating. What kind of heart damage must his mother have had in order for her to do this to her own son? Had she been abused? Abandoned? What had her life been like as a girl growing up? In what ways had this upside-down world enslaved her heart so that she would inflict such pain on one whom God had blessed her to bring into the world?

This young man had sex for the very first time when he was in middle school. His uncle, a drug dealer and pimp, forced him to have sex with one of his prosti-tutes. Every time we would get together, this young man's stories broke my heart. As bright as he was, with so much potential, his heart was damaged by other damaged hearts.

How do we respond when we encounter broken people? In this age of social media, I see so many examples of Christians judging lost, hurting, rebellious, and damaged people instead of being representatives of a God who loves them. Every time I would get together with this young man, I would tell him that God loved him, that I loved him, and that there was another way. I tried to connect him to godly families in our church whom he could possibly live with. My wife, Donecia, and I talked about having him move in with us. Unfortunately, I was not able to convince him to leave his damaged home and consider a new start.

After a couple of months had gone by and I didn't see or hear from this young man, eventually I got a call from a chaplain from the county jail. The young man had been arrested and wanted me to come visit him. For what he had done, there was the possibility that he could be charged as an adult and spend a number of years in prison. That afternoon when we met, we spent most of the time with tears in our eyes, two brokenhearted people trying to find the words to share with one another.

I wish I had a better ending to that story. As a young minister at the time, I was still trying myself to understand all the complexities that were going on in our community. I only knew, as I know now, that even when we know the right things, our damaged hearts can keep us from living out God's purpose for our lives.

A damaged heart can deceive and destroy us. And not only us: Our heart problems can keep us from living into the love that God calls us to extend to our neighbors and our enemies.

Dying to the things of this world that contaminate our hearts begins with realizing that we don't have it in our own power to love the way God desires us to love. We must live daily in the reality of God's steadfast love for us. God showers us daily with an amazing love and grace that we don't deserve. It is out of the overflow of God's love upon us that we are empowered to love other people. When we experience God's reconciliation in our hearts, we die to the ways of the world and begin to live into a ministry of reconciling relationships that characterizes the Kingdom of God.

THE WILL SET RIGHT

At the intersection of my thinking and my feelings are the decisions that I make. What must I die to in order for my daily decisions to be more and more in line with the mission of God in the world? To go to this level of Christian formation will require reflecting back on the behavior and decisions of the previous day, week, or month—a self-audit of how I have lived my life.

For many, this is difficult. This type of reflection without a solid foundation in God's love can bring about considerable guilt and shame. People all too easily beat themselves up for ways in which they have behaved outside of God's will and truth for their lives.

God's right-side-up Kingdom isn't powered by guilt and shame. It's God's kindness, after all, that leads to repentance (Romans 2:4). Right-side-up living is steeped in God's grace.

Having grace as our foundation allows us to see our self-audits as an opportunity to seek God for continued change and transformation. We move forward in living as mature Christians by learning and committing ourselves to allow God to work in and through us. I have found that intentionally putting time aside to reflect with God on the decisions I have made over the past month or year is helpful. Prayer walks have been very helpful for me in this area. As I walk, I reflect on decisions that I wish I could do over. I think about things I said that I wish I could take back. As I think on these things, I thank God for his grace and mercy. I realize how God was with me even when I was making decisions out of anxiety, anger, or hurt. Having done this over time, I am now at a place where I sense God's love, forgiveness, and power. Because I sense this on the inside of myself, I really believe that this is the Holy Spirit working on me. God is doing soul surgery through the Holy Spirit, killing guilt and shame and reviving me with love.

Some people are overtaken by guilt and shame when they reflect on bad decisions they've made. This causes them to retreat into isolation instead of seeking moments of intimacy with God in their vulnerability. In isolation we can find ourselves throwing a pity party for ourselves or angrily justifying even more of our bad decisions. When we blame others in order to justify ourselves and our actions, we are in essence committing idolatry—sacrificing someone else for our own ends. Aligning our decision making with God comes about through intentional intimacy with God, not through isolation and idolatry.

The more we allow God's love to kill those parts of our decision making process that are not about him, the more consistently our decision making aligns with God's mission. But the self-audit isn't just negative. Through this process, we also are given the opportunity to see how we arrived at *good* decisions. On my prayer walks I don't just reflect on bad decisions I've made. I use the time to thank God for those decisions I made that allowed me to participate in his mission. This is a practical way of experiencing my own decreasing, so that God might increase in my life (John 3:30).

REMEMBER YOUR BAPTISM

It has been so many years since my baptism, but I still remember it very clearly. I was in middle school at the time. At that time the African American church that I was a part of with my mother and grandmother gathered for worship at a hotel. The church would later begin to rent space in the building of a white Presbyterian congregation that was in decline and looking to move out of the community. Until then, however, our services took place at a hotel, and our baptisms took place at a YMCA pool.

One Sunday morning at the hotel, Pastor Stanley King preached the sermon and called for people to come forward who wanted to give their life to Christ, be baptized, or join the church. I think even my mother and grandmother were surprised when I went forward and stated in front of the whole congregation that I wanted to be baptized. Pastor King asked me whether I knew what that meant. I explained that I believed Jesus had died on the cross for me, and then I told him, "When you become a Christian, you die to your sins so that you can live for God. I want to go into the water to represent my dying to my sins." Pastor King put his arm around me and smiled. He told the church that we would explain more to me later, but that he would look forward to baptizing me.

A few weeks later, on a Sunday afternoon, Pastor King and Reverend John Ryne, the associate pastor, met me at the YMCA in downtown Minneapolis. The pool seemed so large to me. I was scared. I couldn't swim. I still can't swim to this day. But Pastor King assured me that we were in the shallow end and that he would be holding on to me with Reverend Ryne as I went down and came back up.

I closed my eyes and leaned back onto one of Pastor King's large arms. He looked at the congregants there, including my mother, my grandmother, my father, and relatives who hadn't been to church in a long while. He said, "Brother Efrem Smith, I baptize you in the name of the Father, Son, and Holy Spirit." I went down into the water, and I came back up.

When I got out of the pool, my mother was there with a couple of other members of the church. They had towels with them, and they escorted me back to the locker room, where I would change back into my church clothes. I wondered later that evening whether I was truly a different person.

Even as I reflect back on that event all these years later, I believe that something powerful and mysterious happened that day. Now, because this was a black Baptist church, I was taught that what happened in the pool on that day was symbolic: Just as Christ went into a borrowed tomb upon his death and then came out of that tomb alive, we, being dead in sin, go down into the water (a "tomb") and then come up as new beings in Christ. Through baptism we symbolically die with Christ and are raised with Christ. Today as an adult, I am ordained as a minister in denominations that view baptism differently. But whatever our theology— whether we were baptized as infants or adults, or somewhere in between—we all must wrestle with the same question: Are we, as Christians, truly different? Will we live into our baptism today?

One way to say yes to that question is to connect our own baptism to Christ's baptism.

> Then Jesus came from Galilee to the Jordan to John, to be baptized by him. John would have prevented him, saying, "I need to be baptized by you, and do you come to me?" But Jesus answered him, "Let it be so now, for thus it is fitting for us to fulfill all righteousness." Then he consented. And when Jesus was baptized, immediately he went up from the water, and behold, the heavens were opened to him, and he saw the Spirit of God descending like a dove and coming to rest on him; and behold, a voice from heaven said, "This is my beloved Son, with whom I am well pleased."
> *Matthew 3:13-17*

Jesus' baptism supernaturally revealed his true identity. God publicly declared that he was the Son of the heavenly Father. Similarly, in our baptism God publicly claimed us as his—dead to the world, alive in him.

Right after his baptism, Christ goes into the wilderness and is tempted by the devil. Having just been claimed as God's Son, his identity is cast into doubt:

"If you are the Son of God" (Matthew 4:3, 5). Jesus' identity is confirmed in his responses—and so is his mission: to wage war against a spiritual enemy for the redemption of his Father's creation. Similarly, my baptism doesn't have to be an artifact of the past; it can inform my present and my future. Daily I can experience being crucified with Christ and being resurrected with Christ. Daily I have an opportunity to die so that I can truly live. I can daily gain a greater understanding of my new identity: Just like Christ, I am the beloved of the Father. Just like Christ, I have the opportunity to wage war against the devil.

We think of taking up our crosses daily as a daily death. But it's more than that. The Cross is a pledge of allegiance. We reject this upside-down world, and we join the battle for a world that is right side up.

> Finally be strong in the Lord and in the strength of his might. Put on the whole armor of God, that you may be able to stand against the schemes of the devil. For we do not wrestle against flesh and blood, but against the rulers, against the authorities, against the cosmic powers over this present darkness, against the spiritual forces of evil in the heavenly places. Therefore take up the whole armor of God, that you may be able to

withstand in the evil day, and having done
all, to stand firm.
Ephesians 6:10-13

We follow Christ into war with our ultimate enemy,
confident of Christ's ultimate victory. When God kills
us softly, he's actually inviting us into our best life.

WE ARE NOT ALONE

My wife's grandfather, Reverend Edward Berry Sr., was
my first mentor when I was starting out as a young
minister. He was the father of eleven children, and
the night when he died, he was surrounded by children and grandchildren singing gospel songs. What a
setting in which to go into glory! Just as Pastor Berry
didn't die alone, our spiritual dying is not meant to
occur in isolation. God is with us in the spiritual-death
process, in the person of the Holy Spirit.

All three of these areas—our minds, our hearts, our
wills—offer us the opportunity to experience the Holy
Spirit more fully within our lives. God has provided us
the Holy Spirit as our Helper, so we are not left on our
own as we die to this upside-down world.

If you love me, you will keep my commandments. And I will ask the Father, and he will
give you another Helper, to be with you

forever, even the Spirit of truth, whom the
world cannot receive, because it neither sees
him nor knows him. You know him, for he
dwells with you and will be in you.
John 14:15-17

This is really about a call to the church to go deeper in
our intimacy with God, to experience in new ways our
identity in Christ and the indwelling of the Holy Spirit.

Some people reject God because of their own rebelliousness, hard-heartedness, pride, and arrogance.
Some people have yet to hear the gospel presented
to them. Some, though, may be rejecting Christianity
because the Christianity they see is counterfeit. Why
would people be drawn to a movement that seems to
be racist, sexist, arrogant, judgmental, selfish, unforgiving, and power-hungry? Why would people go to
church to hear a sermon that sounds more like what
they would hear on a cable news channel or at a political rally? They live daily in a world of violence, judgment, consumerism, and materialism. They need the
love, grace, truth, justice, compassion, and transformation of God to come to bear on their upside-down
circumstances. They need the church to be a refuge of
healing, reconciliation, and empowerment. They need
to be delivered from the upside-down world that's killing them into a right-side-up world that gives them
new life. And we can join Christ in welcoming them

into that world. And the Holy Spirit guides us as we live in testimony to that world. Isn't that worth dying for?

QUESTIONS FOR REFLECTION AND DISCUSSION

Reflect on moments in your life when you felt like you were dying in your soul. What were the circumstances? What did you find yourself feeling and thinking? What decisions did you make? How did you get through it?

When have you experienced the liberation of God killing you softly?

How does regularly dying to yourself help you grow in spiritual health and maturity?

5

A CHILD SHALL LEAD US: THE PARADOX OF CHRISTIAN MATURITY

WHEN I WAS A CHILD, I spent a lot of time dreaming of becoming an adult. I saw adulthood as a life of freedom. You could do whatever you wanted. As a child I had to ask my parents' permission before I could go outside and play. I had to ask my parents' permission to have friends over to the house. I couldn't even go to bed when I wanted to; my parents set my bedtime. I looked up to the adults around me because I believed they represented the power of freedom. I was envious of them because it seemed no one told them what to do.

I wanted this adult life. I saw adulthood as an adventure that I couldn't wait to take on.

When I became an adult, I thought, I would decide what I wanted to do and when I would do it. I wouldn't have to ask permission for anything. I would stay out as late as I wanted to. I would eat ice cream for breakfast if I wanted to. I would fall asleep with the television on.

I must admit that as a child I first looked up to pastors because they seemed to have so much freedom and power. The black pastor said whatever he or she felt about race and injustice. The black pastor wore the best suits. The black pastor drove the best cars. People looked up to the black pastor. The greatest African American leader who had ever lived, in my mind— Dr. Martin Luther King Jr.—was a black pastor. Many African Americans in politics, such as Walter Fauntroy (a founding member of the Congressional Black Caucus) and Floyd Flake (a congressman from New York) were also ministers. Two black pastors, Jesse Jackson and Al Sharpton, ran for president while I was growing up. When I first wrestled with the notion of whether I was called to be a minister, I must admit that I was tempted by the power and freedom that seemed to come with the role.

I don't believe I was the only kid who couldn't wait to become an adult. I'm probably raising a couple of kids in my own home now who feel this way. But isn't this the world we live in? Many people dream of careers where they are the boss. Some dream of starting their own business. Some dream of political power, of one day being mayor, governor, or president. To be a billionaire is, in the minds of many, to have ultimate freedom, power, and control. The freedom to do want you want is a widespread desire in our world. But the dream of freedom can sometimes degrade into a desire for control and power.

I was excited in the fall of 1988 when I began my first year as a college student at Saint John's University in Collegeville, Minnesota. I was about to experience what it meant to be an adult, what it meant to be free. I was going to eat whatever I wanted, stay out as late as I wanted, and talk on the phone as long as I wanted. But I eventually came to realize that my freedom was still limited. As much as I wanted to go out into the parking lot outside my dorm at 2 a.m. and yell, "I'm free!", I soon would realize that doing so could get me in trouble. As much as I wanted to talk on the phone all the time, I came to realize that my grades would suffer if I did.

Freedom is good. Freedom is biblical. In the book of Exodus we see God liberating the Jews from slavery in Egypt, and Christ declared that he came to set captives free (Luke 4:18). We are given power and authority by Christ (Matthew 10:1) and are empowered by the Holy Spirit (Acts 1:8). But the freedom the Bible promises also gives us questions to wrestle with:

- What does freedom look like in an upside-down world?
- How should a Christian use the freedom, power, and control they come to have in the upside-down world?
- How does the freedom and power of others in an upside-down world affect us as Christians?

The journey toward answering these questions begins with our understanding of our true identity as Christians—why we exist and what we are to do in this life. Living in an upside-down world can cause desires of the flesh—pride, rebelliousness, and selfishness—to come into play. But these are not qualities that characterize Christians. What does characterize Christians is *childlikeness*.

In Christ we have become the beloved children of God, so we are to approach God as children.

At the time the disciples came to Jesus, saying, "Who is the greatest in the kingdom of heaven?" And calling to him a child, he put him in the midst of them and said, "Truly, I say to you, unless you turn and become like children, you will never enter the kingdom of heaven. Whoever humbles himself like this child is the greatest in the kingdom of heaven.
Matthew 18:1-4

Becoming a child is our entrance into heaven, and the impetus for the work of heaven showing up in our lives here and now.

Christ was once approached by some children— something that seemed to annoy his adult followers. They had a revolution to focus on and didn't need any children distracting them from that very adult work. But Christ told them that to truly follow God was to become like one of those children: "Let the little children come to me and do not hinder them, for to such belongs the kingdom of heaven" (Matthew 19:14).

When Jesus was speaking these words, children were seen, for the most part, as second-class citizens. Children didn't have power or control. Even today, where children are given more value, they have no real voice, influence, or power. They are vulnerable. They need to be taken care of. They need to be protected. Their vocabulary is limited, and they can only handle so much. How could the Kingdom of God come on earth as it is in heaven through an army that thought like children? How could any follower of Jesus lead an effective revolution by acting like a child?

Jesus' words about children would seem like an upside-down concept indeed! But Christ establishes our identity and purpose as being childlike. We come before God as vulnerable beings. We are not fully in control of everything around us. In many ways our pursuit of freedom has been futile.

On the other hand, as we live our lives before God as beloved children, we come to realize that second-class citizenship is not the way of the Kingdom of God; it is the way of this upside-down world. In a right-side-up world, God believes in children. He calls the children to come unto him and invites them into his mission. The Bible is full of stories of God using children and youth to do incredible and amazing things.

- God uses David to kill a giant.
- God uses Esther to save a people.
- God uses Jeremiah to speak truth.
- God uses Timothy to plant churches.

God will use young people as right-side-up agents of transformation. This is at the heart and foundation of World Impact, the missions organization I am privileged to serve and lead. World Impact was incorporated as an urban Christian missions organization in 1971, but its roots go back to the mid-1960s. Keith Phillips was an urban ministry leader at the time. At just sixteen years old, Keith was a college student at UCLA and an inner-city Bible club leader for Youth for Christ in Los Angeles. His very beginnings in ministry show how God can raise up young heroes to advance his Kingdom. But this wasn't the norm for ministry leadership then or now. How many sixteen-year-olds are given the opportunity to be a local parachurch ministry leader in a major city like Los Angeles? Many would assume a teenager is not ready for that type of responsibility, and Keith himself admitted, in his 1975 book *They Dare to Love the Ghetto*, that way back then he was still very naive in his understanding of ministry. He also was in a ministry context that was foreign to his upbringing.

> It started in September, 1964. . . . [I] began my routine of driving into the ghetto after completing my morning classes in Westwood.
>
> Urban America was a different world than the distinctly white, middle-class one where I had grown up. If a black man or a brown man walked into my community, he stuck out like a sore thumb. Mothers gathered their children a little closer to them.

Keith was white and hadn't grown up in a predominantly black and inner-city context. He may have been in over his head, but why wouldn't that be the case? He was just a kid.

Even though he was young in years, though, he was bold enough to venture into the Los Angeles community known as Watts during the 1965 riots.

> The first time I drove into Watts I was afraid, skeptical of so many Blacks heavily concentrated in one area. I felt like an outsider in a

human prison yard. I caught myself looking
down on these creatures who were notorious
for prostitution, narcotics, theft, and violence.

Keith's words are somewhat startling, at least for me
as an African American, as he describes black people
as "creatures." The systemic racism across the United
States in the 1960s sheds light on the language of
Keith's initial narration: He was conditioned by the
social matrix of race as a system, and his language
reflected that matrix—one of the visible signs that
we live in an upside-down world. Keith's words and
his preliminary reaction to the ministry context God
put him in can be interpreted as prejudice, but he
was a kid and a product of his upbringing, and God
desired to use him. God uses children, even those
with a limited understanding of other cultures and
ethnicities.

Keith goes on to describe how his initial feelings as
a teenager in a new ministry environment changed
over time.

As the months passed, an astonishing thing
happened. The fear turned to compassion. The
hate that stemmed from fear started to wane. It
wasn't sudden. There was no thunderbolt from
heaven. Warm feelings were growing between
me and the YFC kids.

By the world's standards, you could make the case that because of his age (and the prejudices of his upbringing), Keith wasn't qualified to do the work he was doing. And yet God had called him and was using him. God was doing soul surgery on Keith, softly killing the presuppositions he had about urban communities and African Americans in particular so that he could develop into the ministry leader God wanted him to be.

Could it be that Keith was more available for God to mold and shape him because he came into ministry so young? People who already perceive themselves as qualified and deserving of a position or opportunity may be less open to God's soul surgery. There is a saying that you can't teach old dogs new tricks. I don't believe that saying is true in all cases, but the older you get, the more experience you get, and the more you are promoted, the easier it is to believe that you don't need to change. This upside-down world can trick people into believing that they have "arrived," that who they are now is fixed and final, and they're not going to change. This is upside-down thinking, not childlike faith.

Keith's childlike faith may have been his greatest asset as a young leader. It may have been what led him into an experience that other urban ministry leaders who were much older were avoiding. Maybe someone much older wouldn't have been able to be molded and shaped the way Keith was by God. Keith began the work of what would ultimately become World Impact by calling other students from local Christian colleges to join him as urban missionaries in Los Angeles. A mantra of "Come die with me in the city" became the entrance into the urban mission field.

In the beginning these mostly white young people would raise the question, "What does this ragtag army of white missionaries know about ministry in a predominantly black urban setting?" And in fact they probably knew very little, if anything. They probably came just like Keith, naive and with prejudices. But they were willing to die—to allow God to kill them softly as they brought the gospel to unchurched urban communities in Los Angeles and later to other cities across the country. Of course urban communities throughout the United States are blessed with a strong African American church presence, but the birth of World Impact among those young people demonstrates that God does not require experts to accomplish his mission: He will meet us at the point of our naïveté and even our prejudices, and use us in his work if we come to him in childlike faith.

World Impact began its work by evangelizing and discipling the unreached urban poor in America through Bible clubs and discipleship home groups, mainly directed at children and youth. Later holistic ministry initiatives, based on the felt needs of the community, would be developed: thrift stores, mobile health clinics, Christian schools, and the like. As urban youth who came to Christ and were being discipled graduated from high school, some came on staff with World Impact—young, passionate, and open to being used by God to transform their own neighborhoods. In this, God was taking two groups that had been divided by race and was building them into a reconciled, Christ-centered, multiethnic army of right-side-up missionaries. They were dying together so that they might collectively advance the Kingdom of God.

Recently I experienced the blessing of attending a reunion in Los Angeles of some former missionaries of World Impact from the early days. This group of black, white, and Asian brothers and sisters had hair that had changed from the 1970s fashions of shoulder-length or Afro to gray or nonexistent. Over a meal, they reminisced about their time on staff. They talked about the mistakes they made, the crazy things they said, the ways they offended one another, and how much they had come to love one another. Though this was a room full of older adults, there was a childlike spirit in the room as they reflected on the ways in which God had transformed them years ago when they were young. I was energized by their stories and was so glad to be a part of this ministry.

Today, World Impact continues its work in urban communities across the country and through partnerships around the world. Along with evangelism, discipleship, and ministries of compassion and justice, there are key initiatives such as the facilitation of urban church-planting movements and the training of indigenous urban leaders. The global-ends statement of World Impact is "the empowered urban poor advancing the Kingdom of God in every city through the local church." We believe that the poor, marginalized, under-resourced, and incarcerated should be able to participate in the great commission just like anyone else.

Just as World Impact began through an army of what could be described as young, inexperienced, and unqualified urban missionaries, the urban poor carry their own questionable stigmas. But we must remember that Christ, who called us to have childlike faith, himself came to earth poor and marginalized. The educated, resourced, and qualified questioned whether anything or anyone of significance could come from Christ's hometown (John 1:46). The poor, the rebellious, and the incarcerated have to navigate an upside-down world that questions their ability to be leaders. World Impact is committed to the empowerment of the young and marginalized because this is what God is committed to.

One man I know, Roosevelt, would say that he was once a thug, a gangster who sought to be feared on urban streets. His upbringing would be described as the urban poor. But God brought about a revolutionary change in Roosevelt's heart. He not only became a Christian but began to sense that God could use his life to make a difference in the urban context. He began to explore a call to ministry as a pastor. He recently graduated from World Impact's Urban Ministry Institute (TUMI) and became senior pastor of a historic African American church in Wichita, Kansas. This in and of itself is a powerful testimony, but there is something else that is amazing to me. When I first met Roosevelt, I would have never guessed that he had the background he does. And I wouldn't have guessed that he held such a prestigious position in his church today. I have met some pastors who come across as arrogant and can't wait to brag about the churches they pastor and how many members they have. Not Roosevelt. He is so humble, down-to-earth, and gentle. He has a child-like faith and a demeanor that God is still working on him. God is still doing soul surgery on Roosevelt, still killing him softly every day, and Roosevelt is still growing as a result. I'm sure that Roosevelt would admit that he's not perfect and that there are areas where he can grow, but he seems satisfied with simply being God's beloved child. This is what being a right-side-up person in this upside-down world looks like.

We must be willing to keep seeing ourselves as God's beloved children. This will be messy indeed, because it goes against the grown-up posture that we are taught to pursue in this world. There are some places, though, where we can learn about being God's beloved children by reflecting back on our own childhoods.

A CHILD IN AWE

When I was a child, I was curious about many things. I would sometime just sit in my backyard and look up in awe at the blue sky and the white clouds. I was in awe of grass, butterflies, and birds.

But then I got older. And it seems that the older I got, the more my sense of awe began to diminish. I became less focused on being awestruck and more focused on becoming awe-inspiring.

It took me so long after becoming a Christ follower to get that awe back. Now, as I venture more deeply into the life of a beloved child of God, I am in awe again—in awe of God's creation and in awe of the growing intimacy I experience with God. I am a different kind of child now, an otherworldly kind of child.

As beloved children of God, we never outgrow him. God is the King of kings. God is all-powerful, all-knowing, and over all things. I will never get taller than God. I will never match the strength, power, love, grace, and wisdom of God. To follow Christ is to accept this childlike relationship with God.

A childlike posture can begin with how we spend time alone with God. One of the struggles I have had over the years has been trying to figure out what devotional time looks like for a grown, seminary-trained pastor and organizational leader. I felt this pressure to have a significant plan with big outcomes that described my time with God.

If some well-known ministry leader talked about spending time with God up in the mountains, I thought that was what I needed to do. But I don't like spending time in the mountains that much.

If someone fasted for a whole month, I thought that to truly be God's child I had to fast for a month. But when I struggled to fast for three days, I felt like a failure.

I feared that I wasn't as spiritual as the other leaders I was reading about or hearing from. But then, during one of my doctor of ministry classes, a leader from a large missions organization shared how he spends a day a month alone with God. Before he even began, I prepared myself for the extraordinary examples he would provide. To my surprise he talked about spending time at his favorite coffee shop, going on walks, listening to jazz, eating at his favorite buffet, and taking naps.

I think my mouth was open long enough to swallow a fly if it had been buzzing around my head. Weren't these examples too simple, too childlike? They didn't sound very spiritual. But he shared how spending time with God in this way gave him space to reflect on a variety of things: family-of-origin issues, ways in which he was leading, and the anger he had carried around in his heart for years. He had found his own personal rhythm for time with God, and God was killing him softly on a regular basis.

I was empowered by his words to find my own personal rhythms for spending time alone with God. I needed my own ways to experience God as "Daddy" and to grow deeper in my identity as his well-loved son. I needed ways to experience a big God that were personally meaningful for me.

Right-side-up people are mindful of how big God is. We are mindful of what a big deal the mission of God is. But this takes place in ways that are intimate and personally impactful, not in ways tailored to make other adults see us as super-spiritual. My time with God may seem silly to others, but it's my way of experiencing life as God's beloved child.

A RECONCILING CHILD

Another thing I remember about my childhood is the playground. I loved to play, whether it was recess time at elementary school, going to the park in my neighborhood, or Saturdays in my backyard. I had a number of friends whom I played with—school friends at recess, neighborhood friends with whom I would meet up at the park, and close friends who would come to my house. I played kickball, football, double-dutch, and basketball. My friends were ethnically and racially diverse: John was white, Mike was black, Jay was biracial, and Ramona was Indian. I didn't see myself as better or worse than any of them. It wasn't that I didn't recognize that some of my friends looked different from me. I wasn't colorblind. Sometimes we talked about our skin color and physical features, but not in an oppressive or divisive way. We were our own little community.

It wasn't until I became older that I became more aware of the unreconciled world that I lived in. By the time I was in high school I began to personally feel the effects of living in a racialized society. I wasn't called a nigger until I was a college student, when a car full of drunk white students yelled it from a car window one evening.

I don't believe children are born racist. But people of all ethnicities are born into a sinful world that can mold us into prejudiced, oppressive, and discriminating people. I don't believe white people are born racist, but they are born into an upside-down world that can mold them within a web of white privilege, even white supremacy. It takes a childlike faith for Christians to truly live in our racialized world as ambassadors of reconciliation.

The racism and racist structures that characterize our upside-down world cannot be dismantled without a collective commitment to reconciliation, justice, and transformation. The path to such a commitment is through living as the beloved children of God.

It is disheartening that the Christian church is still one of the most visible examples of the racial divide in the United States. How can we show this upside-down world the love of God if we aren't living as the beloved church of Christ? Every Christian should reflect deeply on whom we share life with. Who are our friends? Who is in our inner circle? If we work for a church, para-church, or missions organization, whom are we on staff with? Whom are we on the playground with?

Wherever possible, the church should be a picture of the Kingdom of God: Christ-centered, multiethnic, multicultural, multilingual (Revelation 5:9). There are some instances in which there is still a need for ethnic-specific or homogeneous congregations. If the neighborhood surrounding a local church is predomi-nantly Hispanic, for example, then missionally speak-ing, there is a need for a Hispanic church. When it comes to reaching first-generation immigrant groups with the gospel, ethnic-specific churches make sense. And in light of racial disparities in the areas of edu-cation, employment, incarceration, and economic development, there remains a distinct ministry for a black church. But in an increasingly multiethnic and multicultural world, there is an urgent need for more churches that provide a sneak preview of heaven.

Even in the case of ethnically homogeneous, mission-directed churches, we still need to collaborate across lines of race, denomination, and socioeconomic status in order to achieve greater Kingdom advancement and transformation. We need churches to build bridges of reconciliation, ensuring that although we function as individual, local congregations, we do not lose sight of our participation in the larger church of God in the world—and that our individual congregations receive the blessing and empowerment that come from being the beloved children of God. There is a blessing awaiting white churches when they fellowship and partner with black churches. There is a blessing for black churches when they fellowship with and partner with Hispanic churches. There is a blessing for Hispanic churches when they fellowship with and partner with Asian churches. There is a blessing for suburban churches when they connect with and learn from urban churches. There is a blessing for megachurches when they connect with and learn from storefront churches. But it takes a childlike faith to believe that we can be blessed by one another.

There are many ways in which we can live out being the beloved community of God's children. Reconciliation within the church probably won't be led day in and day out by pastors. It's going to take Christians who seek to build childlike relationships across racial lines on their jobs, at their schools, and in the neighborhoods where they live.

In the summer of 2016, yet another tragedy struck the United States in the divide between police departments and African American communities. The deaths of Alton Sterling in Baton Rouge, Louisiana, and Philando Castile in Saint Paul, Minnesota, at the hands of police officers were followed by the murders of police officers in Dallas and Baton Rouge. In the upside-down world, political and media rhetoric poured gasoline on the fire of racial tensions. Some blamed President Obama, others the candidates of the two major parties running to be the next president, and still others the Black Lives Matter movement for the heightened racial tensions. While the flames of racial division were burning, a reconciling event took place in Wichita, Kansas. Members of the local chapter of Black Lives Matter and members of the Wichita Police Department decided to put on a community cookout in a park. Instead of violence, yelling, and division, for an afternoon there was laughing, eating, dancing, playing, and praying. Yes, praying. I was so moved when I saw the pictures of Black Lives Matter members and police officers standing in a circle holding hands, with their heads bowed. If only there were more childlike moments like that. If only a childlike cookout would lead to childlike humility, apologies, forgiveness, reform, and justice. Maybe our grown-up strategies are the problem. Upside-down solutions won't fix upside-down problems.

Maybe revolutions of reconciliation don't begin in the streets but over potluck meals, backyard barbecues, and community cookouts, with real conversations that involve really listening to one another's stories. When we were kids at the playground, it didn't matter what color the other kids were in the sandbox, on the swing set, or coming down the slide. We learned to share, to take turns, and to build community. Maybe we grown folks need to rediscover the spirit of the playground.

THE IMITATING CHILD

When I was a child, I loved imitating powerful, famous, and heroic figures. I'd grab my football, run out into the backyard, and pretend to be Franco Harris of the Pittsburgh Steelers, Tony Dorsett of the Dallas Cowboys, or Doug Williams of the Tampa Bay Buccaneers. I would grab a pillowcase, tie it around my neck like a cape, and then run outside pretending I was Batman or Superman. I became so good at imitating James Brown that I had my own version: I called him Vernon Brown. I would take requests from my relatives at large family gatherings. Imitation, for me at least, was a central part of childhood.

Each of us is a unique, precious, and anointed creation of God. We have gifts, talents, and passions that are unique to who we are and how we are wired. Nevertheless, we are called by the Scriptures to be imitators of Christ. This world ought to look at us, individually and collectively, and see aspects of who Christ is. We must explore what imitating Christ looks like. We must also reflect regularly on our lives and ask ourselves whether people can tell that we are imitating Christ: "Therefore be imitators of God, as beloved children. And walk in love, as Christ loved us and gave himself up for us, a fragrant offering and sacrifice to God" (Ephesians 5:1-2).

Imitating Christ is an act of surrender, allowing Christ to live in us through the Holy Spirit. It's about giving God permission to continually shape our decisions and our behavior. Our lives won't be perfect, but who God is will more and more be perfected in our being.

Imitating Christ is the way to deeper intimacy with the heavenly Father, which itself is the way to experiencing greater identity in Christ. As I imitate Christ, I am empowered by the Holy Spirit living in me to become a change agent like Christ for this upside-down world. And all the while I experience more and more the right-sided life of a citizen of God's Kingdom and a beloved child in God's family.

Awe, reconciliation, and the imitation of Christ: These all are ways in which we are shaped by God through a childlike faith. But no discussion of childlike faith would be complete without a discussion of how God uses discipline to kill us softly and resurrect us into Kingdom life.

DISCIPLINE AND THE BELOVED CHILD

As I look back on my childhood and my relationship with my earthly parents, I have come to appreciate the times when they disciplined me. It came from the tremendous love they had for me as a child.

Lord knows I didn't appreciate at the time. I grew up in the inner city of Minneapolis. The neighborhoods where I spent a lot of my upbringing became more crime infested as the years went by. Gangs became more prevalent in my community. My parents knew the challenges and dangers outside our door. They loved me and my siblings and wanted to see all of us grow up into productive and successful adulthood. In such a broken community, to keep us on that path, they sometimes had to discipline us.

I want to be sensitive around the issue of discipline. There are children who under the banner of discipline have been abused. We must continually distinguish between healthy discipline born of the love parents have for their children, and instances of parents abusing their roles in the lives of their children. But understood and practiced correctly and biblically, discipline is in fact a means of maturing us.

We have a heavenly Father who loves us greatly. Part of discovering our true purpose is placing ourselves in a position to receive discipline from God. Through God's Word, prayer, and the accountability of other believers in beloved community, we can identify the ways in which our current behavior and attitudes don't align with Christ living in and through us. For a beloved child of God, this type of spiritual discipline is a gift.

The problem with discipline in the upside-down world is that it clashes with our upside-down desire to achieve a status in life where no one can tell us anything. Kingdom love, compassion, truth, and justice compete for our allegiance with more self-serving motivations. Our capacity to extend the love, truth, and grace of God comes into conflict with a political ideology that appeals to our worldly interests. Do we resemble the brokenness, divisiveness, and prejudices of this world more than we want to admit? Spiritual discipline is a way to process this.

I realize that the term "spiritual discipline" could be confused with "spiritual disciplines" such as prayer, fasting, and solitude. There need not be any confusion. Spiritual disciplines are practices that lead to deeper intimacy with God. They shape our Christian formation and help us grow as disciples. Spiritual discipline has a similar result—greater intimacy with God—but its origins are with God, not with us. We practice spiritual disciplines; God practices spiritual discipline on us.

In Scripture, spiritual discipline from God is connected to running a race, or staying the course that God has set for us.

Therefore, since we are surrounded by so great
a cloud of witnesses, let us also lay aside every
weight, and sin which clings so closely, and
let us run with endurance the race that is set
before us, looking to Jesus, the founder and
perfecter of our faith, who for the joy that was
set before him endured the cross, despising the
shame, and is seated at the right hand of the
throne of God. . . .

And have you forgotten the exhortation that
addresses you as sons?

"My son, do not regard lightly the discipline of the
      lord,
   nor be weary when reproved by him.
For the Lord disciplines the one he loves,
   and chastises every son whom he receives."

It is for discipline that you have to endure. God
is treating you as sons. For what son is there
whom his father does not discipline? If you
are left without discipline, in which all have
participated, then you are illegitimate children
and not sons.
Hebrews 12:1-8

Those who were receiving this word from God on running the race before them were facing oppression,

affliction, and suffering in their upside-down world. It would take an amazing faith to stay the course in such circumstances. They would need the strength to endure. In this light God, in disciplining us, is like a personal trainer.

I decided about eight years ago that I wanted to get in better shape. At the time, I worked out very little. Sometimes I would work out at the YMCA. My wife encouraged me to start working out with a personal trainer. The first time I worked out with Mike, I really wasn't interested in another session. I liked walking on the treadmill and lifting weights. Mike wanted me to try new workout routines and use different equipment that I wasn't comfortable with. It was painful, and I felt like I was going to throw up. I had my own plans for working out. I had to be honest, however: I wasn't really getting into better shape doing things my own way.

Working out with Mike not only led me to trying different workout routines; we also started talking about my diet. When it came to my eating habits, I really lacked discipline. I ate fast food for lunch just about every day during the week. Mike had different plans for me.

Over time, I was able to do things I couldn't believe. I was able to lift more weight. I was able to start running on the treadmill and discovered I was faster than I thought. Mike was affirming at times, and at other times he would sort of chastise me. He pushed me to think differently and live differently. In a manner of speaking, he was disciplining me.

By giving Mike permission to challenge me on the way I was living my life, I injected discipline into my life. I listened to his counsel and began to see good results. Though I live in a different state now and don't have Mike as my personal trainer anymore, I still apply the lessons I learned from him to how I live. I slip into bad eating habits here and there, but not the way I used to. I actually desire to eat better. I now am more open to discover new workout routines that can lead to a healthier me.

What if we allowed God to become our great personal trainer? What if we allowed God to push us— through the Scriptures, through other believers, and through times of prayer and meditation? When we navigate this upside-down world through our own instincts, we don't see significant spiritual results. But with God's affirmation (and even his rebuking), we can become stronger. The God of the universe is also a steadfast, loving Father. He uses spiritual discipline to empower us to run the race of our true life purpose, to help us become more and more like Christ. When we remember that we are God's beloved children, accepting discipline from him is not a burden but a gift.

STILL IN NEED OF A FATHER

I have learned over the years that there is a lot of my father in me. Even though there was a time when I was much younger and talked about ways that I would *never* become like him, I consider myself fortunate now that there are many valuable traits reproduced in me from my father. Like him, I can get up early in the morning without an alarm clock. Like him, there is a courage and healthy boldness that rises out of me at times. Like him, I'm very observant of people and situations. My father is in me in many ways.

I still find myself needing my father. The ways in which I need him has changed over the years, of course, but I need him all the same. I need his wisdom. I need to simply hear his voice. I need to be in his presence. Even though I am a grown man, I sometimes get this sort of childlike feeling where I need my dad.

I live in California now, and my parents live in Florida, so I don't get to see my dad as much. But I talk to him on the phone just about every week. When a week goes by and my dad and I don't talk, I feel it and miss it. I don't feel guilt or shame when we don't talk; I just miss talking to him. I desire to have time with him. I gain strength from my dad. I gain wisdom from him. After talking to my dad, I find myself reflecting on my purpose, character, and decision making.

I trust my dad, and he has my heart. I know he loves me. At the end of every conversation we have by phone, he tells me he loves me. But even if he didn't, I would still know he does. I feel it on the inside.

Every time we talk, my dad asks me how Donecia is doing. He asks me how our two daughters are doing. He is mindful of them. Then there are the times when we just talk about sports or music. He makes me laugh. It's an incredible relationship. I wish that every son had a relationship with his earthly father the way I do. But we live in an upside-down, sinful, and broken world. I don't take the relationship I have with Mr. Forice Smith for granted.

Some nights I have dreams, and my father is in them. Sometimes I am an adult and he is his current age, and other times I am a child and he is a younger man again. I wake up from these dreams with a sense of joy and peace.

All that I am describing about my earthly father, as powerful and meaningful as it is, is nothing in comparison to the kind of intimate relationship the heavenly Father wants with me. God is not visible like my earthly father. God's voice doesn't come across like my father's over the phone. But all that considered, it is possible by faith to experience a deeper, childlike relationship with God that strengthens and empowers us, a relationship that brings more clarity to our life mission.

Being a child of God is not just about our experiences alone with him; it's also about how we carry God's name in the places we go. My earthly father was known by a number of people in the community where I grew up. If I went to the local barbershop or community center, another person might see me and say to someone, "That's Forice Smith's son right there." How I carried myself, how I talked to other people and behaved, were a reflection on how my dad was raising me. What if we lived like this as children of God? Can people tell by the way we live that we represent our Father in heaven? A child of God ought to represent God well.

Now, as a child of Forice Smith, I can point to times when I didn't represent him well. And I don't know whether we ever in this upside-down world perfectly represent God. But we should be ever mindful both of the responsibility of being beloved children of God, and of the Holy Spirit in us, equipping us in this effort. The discipline of God is a loving act of killing us softly, whittling away at our sin and brokenness so that we more fully and consistently reflect God's image.

As I have made more room in my life to spend with God, I have gained a greater understanding of who I am. And there are moments when I have a feeling on the inside of being beloved by God. There are moments when I sense God's presence surrounding me. Even if I am alone, I realize in these intimate moments that I am not alone. I begin to see things differently. I receive wisdom, revelation, and insight. I imagine different ways that I could improve in how I care for people and how I can listen more. I begin to imagine what God could do through me.

Sometimes these thoughts are overwhelming and intimidating. I wonder whether it's possible for a God so mighty to use someone like me. I think about things I've said and done that I wish I hadn't, and at times feelings of doubt and inadequacy set in. But then the almighty personal trainer, the creator of the universe, mysteriously touches my soul. I imagine this is my experiencing God through the Holy Spirit.

I have a long way yet to go, but I want to live in this childlike relationship with my Father on a regular basis. When I miss concentrated, intimate time with God, I don't need to feel guilty; I just need to acknowledge that I miss my Daddy.

So many Christians are trying so hard to be grown up that it hinders our ability to advance the Kingdom of God. Our attempts at trying to control our lives limit our ability to make Christ known. I wonder whether the church remains so segregated, so stripped of awe, and so unlike Christ because we are so busy trying to be grown up, and capitulating to the "grown-up" values of an upside-down world.

Citizenship in the Kingdom of God is connected to being childlike. Jesus said so. We are not just a part of an eternal Kingdom; we are part of a great family, brothers and sisters sharing the same loving Father. Armed with this love and with childlike faith, we become an army, advancing the right-side-up Kingdom of God.

QUESTIONS FOR REFLECTION AND DISCUSSION

What did you dream of becoming when you were a child?

What do you miss about being a child?

Where in your life today can you begin to experience a more childlike faith?

6

LOVE IS OUR ONLY WEAPON: HOW GOD WINS

I HAVE BEEN MARRIED to Donecia Norwood-Smith for over twenty years. We first met when I was a high school sophomore and she was a freshman, but it wasn't until my senior year that she really caught my attention.

I was attracted to Donecia initially for three reasons: She was very pretty; she was a Christian; and she was serious about her studies. She was so serious about school that most of the time, if I wanted to see her, I had to go to the library.

One day as I was getting ready to head home, I told her that I would talk to her later. "How can you talk to me later," she responded, "if you don't have my phone number?" That question changed everything. From then on we talked every day in the library after school, and just about every evening on the phone. Some days I would walk her home after school.

Love is a powerful thing. It takes over your insides. I felt love for Donecia in my gut. It was hard to describe, but it was there all the same.

Then came the day when Donecia broke up with me. We always walked through a park on our way home, past a basketball court, a baseball field, and a series of park benches. Suddenly she stopped walking and asked me to sit with her on one of the park benches. She told me that she had three priorities: God, family, and school. Our relationship was messing up those priorities; she thought that we should focus on being friends for a while.

Of course I was devastated. I was in love, and I was experiencing heartbreak for the first time. Love is so powerful that when you sense you are losing it, it hurts.

Well, I was determined to get Donecia back as my girlfriend—but not for the reasons that you might think. I wanted revenge.

For months I worked hard to get us back together again. I tried to show her that God, family, and school were high priorities for me, as well. Eventually my plan worked, and we renewed our dating relationship. We were together again for just a couple of months when

I broke up with Donecia on the eve of my graduation day over the phone. I told her that I thought we should just be friends.

I wanted Donecia to feel the pain I felt when she broke up with me. I wanted to hurt her, to have her feel the loss of love that I had felt. Oh, the mind of teenage boys!

It only took a few weeks for me to learn that my plan hadn't worked out so well. I thought I would feel good inside for getting my revenge on Donecia, but I had underestimated the power of love. I thought about her all the time. I missed talking on the phone. I missed going to movies with her. I missed eating meals with her in the mall food court.

I worked all summer trying to let her know that I regretted breaking up with her and that I wanted us to be together, but she wasn't hearing any of what I was trying to say. It wasn't until the week before I was to leave for college that she agreed to get back together. A year later, she would attend college in the same area as me. By my senior year in college, we were engaged to be married. On February 13, 1993, Donecia became my wife.

Married life has not always been easy, but love has gotten us through. I have come to realize that it is the love of God that has truly empowered and sustained us. God knows how to love Donecia better than I do. God's love, I've learned, is a strong defense against the threats marriages face in this upside-down world: hedonism, selfishness, pride, unforgiveness, and a culture of violence in which women are used, abused, or exploited to indulge the fleshly desires of men. In this world, where we're encouraged to look out for number one, a marriage that stands the test of time is one that has been fought for.

God's love has been a weapon in the battle for our marriage. But its power extends beyond the marital relationship. God's love empowers us to fight for our spiritual health, for the advancement of God's Kingdom, and for the countless lost and marginalized people who are unable to fight for themselves.

FIGHTING FOR YOUR CHRISTIAN LIFE

When we think of fighting, we tend to think first of fear. The anticipation of being hurt, abused, exploited, or killed evokes in us a "fight or flight" response: If we don't fight, we'll be overtaken, and if we can't win a fight, we might as well run.

In an upside-down world, fear comes first. We assess the risk we face, and then we decide what weapon we will use to mitigate the risk. Some people take self-defense classes, and others carry pepper spray. Some people don't go anywhere without a knife or a gun. In an upside-down world, we expect acts of violence, and we prepare ourselves accordingly.

Even people of faith accept the upside-down norm of violence. Some evangelical leaders have encouraged Christians to respond to the threat of violence with violence, at the level of global conflict and even at the local level. Pastors have posted pictures of themselves holding military-grade assault weapons, daring the government to come and take their weapons. Many of these same leaders would have criticized groups such as the Black Panthers in the 1960s and 1970s for carrying guns in their communities as a protest against police brutality.

Of course, real threats of violence should be taken seriously, and Christians are not wrong to consider how they would defend themselves against attack. But a preoccupation with the threat of violence too easily becomes an obsession with violence and the acceptance of an upside-down notion that violence is invariably the best means to solve conflict. We give in to the fear of being harmed or killed, and that fear itself begins to kill us.

God's primary weapon for Christians in this upside-down world is love. It's God's primary weapon for us because it is God's primary weapon for himself.

Yes, it's true that we see places in Scripture where God is angry, where God judges, and even where God uses violence. Read the first half of the unfolding drama of the Scriptures, and you'd start to suspect that God is at war with the world. But read the second half, and you see God overcome not the people he created but death itself (1 Corinthians 15:54-55). You see God cast out fear with perfect love (1 John 4:18); you see God inaugurate a world without death or pain (Revelation 21:4). And then look more closely at the first half of the Scriptures, and you see that God's love—love for his creation, love for the people created in his image—is never not there. The Scriptures go so far as to say that God is love (1 John 4:8).

The Bible does describe a war taking place. Satan, in the form of a serpent, launches the first strike against the Creator of the universe in Genesis 3. In triggering this war, Satan influences the distortion of creation and humanity. In our sin, we are certainly cobelligerents with Satan in his war against God. But we are also victims of Satan's war, which turns our world upside down and fills our lives with fear.

The ultimate expression of God's love for us is Christ Jesus. He is, if you will, God's weapon of mass destruction against sin. The impact of his life and ministry turns the upside-down world right side up again. But because Jesus is God and God is love, this weapon in the war against Satan doesn't deal in violence. God's strategic attack against Satan and this upside-down world is to give us access to intimate relationship with himself. We are restored to right relationship with God; we are indwelt with Jesus; and we are filled with the Holy Spirit. And so we are empowered to fight for our Christian lives.

We can't put up this fight without first surrendering ourselves to God's love for us. We must live in this love daily. Do you love God? That may come across as a simple or even accusatory question, but the fight for our lives begins here: Receiving God's love daily empowers us to fight.

WE ARE LOVERS AND FIGHTERS

What do we fight for? As God's beloved, we fight for our integrity, character, and purpose in this world. Some people who don't walk in the daily reality of God's love fight for other things. Some people are fighting to get approval from others. Some people are fighting for positions of influence, power, and control. Some are fighting to overcome the fear that would otherwise paralyze them. When we enter into the reality of being beloved by God, however, we begin to recognize the power of love—God's weapon of choice.

God decided a long time ago that our broken and sinful lives were worth fighting for. We begin, then, by loving ourselves as God loves us, and in turn, we begin to love others as God loves them. This, in fact, is what Jesus referred to as the second great commandment: "You shall love your neighbor as yourself" (Matthew 22:39). We can't love our neighbors without loving ourselves first.

God loves you so much that God made a way for

you to be transformed and empowered by his love. Your upside-down life has been set right side up by this liberating love. No matter how upside-down the situation you grew up in or the circumstances you presently find yourself in, God's love empowers you to stay right side up and help turn your neighbors' lives around.

LOVE ADVANCES THE KINGDOM OF GOD

When Christ walked the earth in human form, he declared and demonstrated the Kingdom of God through words and acts of love. When Christ gave mobility to the paralyzed, healed the sick, and spoke evil spirits out of the demonized, he was extending the love of God. In Matthew 9, we see examples of this. As Christ is teaching in a house, a man who is paralyzed is brought in. Christ speaks to him, and the man is given the miraculous ability to walk out of the house on his own, his health and dignity restored. Christ then has a meal with a tax collector, someone who exploited people financially as part of an oppressive system. Such a person was broadly despised by religious leaders, but Christ extended love and fellowship to him. Then Christ was approached by a military official, part of the imperial government that was oppressing the people God had made a historic covenant with. It was the power and weapon of God's love that sent Christ to the funeral of this man's daughter, and God's love that brought his daughter back to life.

But wait, there's more. On the way to the funeral, Christ was touched by a diseased woman. In the culture of that day, if you were a woman, you were already basically a second-class citizen. But if you were diseased, you were an outcast. The assumption was that a woman like this was cursed. It would be best not to get close to a woman like that. Yet Christ put himself in a position to be touched by this woman. He acknowledged her touch. He healed her incurable disease. God's love isn't just an abstract concept: God's love is touchable for the marginalized and the outcast. God's love recognizes and restores the full humanity of people. In an upside-down world—where people are marginalized and oppressed based on their skin color, their gender, and their class—the love of God is a powerful weapon of transformation and empowerment.

The love of God is a weapon in the war against death. It brings new life to those left for dead. So let's use it that way. In this upside-down world there are girls caught in the slavery of human trafficking who have been left for dead. There are people in extreme poverty who have been left for dead. There are people who look like me in America's inner cities who have been left to die as members of street gangs. There are incarcerated people who have been left to die behind bars. There are undocumented immigrants who struggle here and are threatened with deportation back to untenable situations. There are homeless people who have been left to die on the streets and under bridges. We must wage war against this upside-down and broken reality. And our weapon in that battle is love.

As Matthew 9 comes to a close, it's as if Matthew doesn't have enough time to share all the ways in which Christ uses the love of God to advance the Kingdom of God. So he sums it up:

> And Jesus went throughout all the cities and
> villages, teaching in their synagogues and
> proclaiming the gospel of the kingdom
> and healing every disease and every affliction.
> When he saw the crowds, he had compassion
> for them, because they were harassed and
> helpless, like sheep without a shepherd.
> *Matthew 9:35-36*

The meaning behind this word *compassion* is "intestines" or "bowels." You could interpret this as "guts." When God looks at the multitude of people broken, marginalized, and oppressed in this upside-down world, he feels it in his gut.

What else does God feel in his gut? God feels love in his gut because love is at the center of God. Remember, the Bible tells us that God is love.

Christ acknowledges that this upside-down world is filled with paralyzed, diseased, corrupted, demonized, and left-for-dead people. He goes on to call on his followers to take up their divine weapons and join the fight: "The harvest is plentiful, but the laborers are few; therefore pray earnestly to the Lord of the harvest to send out laborers into his harvest" (Matthew 9:37-38).

We are not to simply become citizens of the Kingdom of God and then wait for the day of our supernatural transport into eternity. We are to participate in the advancement of the Kingdom of God right here and right now—to actively demonstrate the way of a world turned right side up.

A privatized or individualized Christian life does not truly reflect citizenship in the Kingdom of God. What does it look like to publicly represent the Kingdom of God? Christ invites us into the discovery of the answer to those questions.

KINGDOM LABORERS

Following Christ is a labor of love, in that it is a life of making God's love public. Christ describes this work as healing the sick, casting out evil spirits, and proclaiming the Kingdom of God. Kingdom laborers are carriers of the gospel and agents of transformation.

To this degree, we are all evangelists. This does

not mean we have to be able to preach evangelistic messages. It means that we extend God's love to the lost and broken around us. We pray for others. We listen to others. We are prepared to speak words of love, healing, and truth in one-on-one conversations with others. We allow others to get close enough to our lives to experience Christ.

Wherever we are in life and whatever career field we are in, we are missionaries. Larry Wiens is a former parachurch ministry leader and business owner. He now leads the San Francisco chapter of the Barnabas Group, a gathering of senior-level executives in the marketplace, who use their skills and talents to help ministries to be more fruitful. He also has a passion and burden for marketplace leaders to see their own businesses and the broader marketplace as a mission field. He believes that the church should be the very place where marketplace leaders are equipped to see where they work as the place to provide a glimpse of the right-side-up world. In too many cases, however, the church only sees marketplace leaders for their giving potential and the business insights they could contribute to the church board. In other cases, these leaders are asked to serve the church in roles that don't fit their gifts, talents, and passions. Of course, there are times when the work of God needs people to serve outside of their primary gifts and talents, but the church's witness in the world suffers from not equipping people to live as right-side-up people where they spend the most time. Our impact in advancing the Kingdom of God has been hindered by not calling people to the mission field of their career field.

Recently, one of our World Impact staff in the San Francisco Bay Area was referred to a business owner through the Barnabas Group who has found his missional calling by hiring people recently released from prison. He has already hired two men who were involved in our urban ministry while incarcerated and have also participated in our re-entry leadership homes. He sets things right by providing an opportunity for the formerly incarcerated to start a new life.

This mission field that we are called to engage as right-side-up people is an ever-increasing multiethnic and multicultural one. The work of a missionary must then involve learning the stories, dreams, and pain of others, cross-culturally—to allow God to dismantle our prejudices and stereotypes across gender, class, and race so that we might extend transformative love and forge reconciliation in sinful and divided situations.

One cannot be a missionary and Kingdom laborer if prejudices contaminate the heart. One cannot be a missionary and not acknowledge the full humanity of all those around them. Prejudice is a form of fear, which is a weapon in the war Satan started against God; the perfect love of God—God's weapon—casts out fear. As we lean into God's love, it becomes possible to stand firmly on the authority and centrality of Scripture and reject prejudice, acknowledging that all human beings are made in the image of God even as all are in need of salvation, transformation, and liberation. God's love for us cultivates God's love in us.

We live in a divided world. Can we truly serve as Kingdom laborers if we are contributing to the division? Is judgment and anger really the solution to racism, sexism, and classism? Is sustained anger and judgment really going to address systemic poverty and injustice? The various social issues of this upside-down world should indeed break our hearts and even provoke righteous anger. But love, reconciliation, and healing action is what will bring the Kingdom of God to bear on these issues.

This doesn't mean that we have to compromise biblical truth; it means that we acknowledge that being known primarily as judgmental and angry with the world works at cross-purposes with our living as evangelists, missionaries, and ambassadors of God's love. Christ looks at the multitude of broken, lost, and sinful people trapped by these issues and both feels and extends compassion, the deepest core of who God is. Christ then invites us to participate in this work.

Living as right-side-up people and beloved children of God is about aligning our lives with the compassion of God. Some Christians respond to social issues with political ideology instead of the revolutionary love of God. Their Kingdom labor is absorbed into an upside-down political agenda, whether on the right or on the left. It pains my heart when influential Christian leaders have an opportunity to say something in order to bring the Kingdom of God to bear upon a social issue, and they end up sounding just like a politician. At its worst, some people use Christian language as a gloss for self-gain and worldly promotion. Divorced from God's love, our work may see some small or short-term success, but ultimately it will devolve into one of those things of the world that is slowly and silently killing us. Even Christians who are politicians professionally should see their role as being missionaries within politics. I would imagine that this is not easy, but this is the messiness of being in this world but not of it (John 17:15-19).

The church is hindered in its Kingdom witness when Christians base their actions in upside-down beliefs. We must continually surrender to the love of God if we want our Kingdom labor to bear Kingdom fruit.

KINGDOM RESPONSIBILITY

Christ came to bring love, liberation, empowerment, and salvation to upside-down people if they are willing to receive it. Christ is the embodiment of the guts of God; he sees oppressed, broken, and lost people as *his* people. As Kingdom laborers in this world, we must take on this same Christ-centered responsibility.

I have spent more than twenty-five years working in urban ministry—as a pastor, as a church planter, and as a director of an urban missions organization. In all those years, one thing I've never done is look at people in an urban context and think of them as "those people." I grew up in the urban context. I have family members and dear friends who are still living in the urban context. When I see urban people who are broken and lost and trapped in an upside-down world, I see *my* people.

Some Christians can't see lost and broken people as their people; they can see them only as part of an opposing army. But this isn't how the Scriptures teach us to see people. The Scriptures teach us that we all are made in the image of God; we all are "harassed and helpless, like sheep without a shepherd" (Matthew 9:36). For the Christian, "my people" cannot be limited; "my people" includes all people.

We must extend ourselves, as God's people, to people who are very different from us. This is what led Christ to eat with tax collectors and other sinners. This is what led Christ to sit at the well with the Samaritan woman. He embodied a revolutionary idea of "my people."

When we surrender ourselves to the love of God, we take responsibility on some level for the harassed and helpless around us. It starts by seeing all people as being made in God's image, just as we are made in God's image. Fueled by this vision and this love for others, we are able take responsibility for the brokenness of this world in some way.

We are not truly able to do this in our own power. Christ calls his followers to what seems like impossible actions. Never mind healing the sick and raising the dead: Can we truly end poverty, racism, sexism, abortion, and human trafficking? Can we even put a major dent in these and other social ills? Yes we can. We are empowered by God to fight these battles, to participate in setting the world right side up again. We don't have to ask permission from this upside-down world to heal, reconcile, liberate, love, and empower. We are given authority from God to go about this Kingdom-advancing work.

Out of our 280 staff at World Impact, 109 of them are part of our Religious Missionary Order (RMO). Having an RMO makes World Impact a missionary form of the church. Our missionaries make a second-level commitment to the mission of the ministry: They go beyond their job description to live as neighbors among the urban poor in cities across America, such as Los Angeles, Fresno, Wichita, Newark, and Dallas. They are like a Protestant version of the Jesuits of the Catholic Church. World Impact is not just where they work; it's also their church community as well. Together, our missionaries form church communities of worship, discipleship, and extended family. World Impact missionaries take vows of simplicity, purity, and submission to the mission. By job description our missionaries may be teachers in one of our Christian schools, church plant movement facilitators, program directors at one of our camp and conference centers, or youth ministers at one of our teen centers. But regardless of the job description, the missionary commitment to the RMO calls them to live in solidarity with the poor, to learn from the poor, and, through a focus on indigenous leadership development, maybe even to serve under them in ministry. The missional call goes beyond just evangelism and discipleship among the urban poor, to being used by God to empower the poor to advance the Kingdom of God in their own communities.

The empowerment of the poor is about seeing poor people the way that God sees them. The initial group of people whom Christ called to follow him weren't privileged religious folks. He called rebels, outcasts, and marginalized and poor people. He told them that they could do greater things than they witnessed him doing, empowered by the Holy Spirit. I often say to our missionaries that the ultimate fruit of our ministry should be that the urban poor are so empowered that they one day look at us and say, "We've got this now—you can leave. We appreciate your love, support, resourcing, and training, but we are ready to lead ministries of transformation here in our own communities." Ultimately, missions is not about the missionary but about the unreached and unchurched embracing a Kingdom responsibility for transformation in this upside-down world.

That said, you don't have to take vows in a religious missionary order to participate in the Kingdom empowerment of others. When I was pastoring the Sanctuary Covenant Church in North Minneapolis a few years ago, we noticed a correlation between incarceration levels in our community and the math scores of third graders in the urban public school. If a kid was doing poorly in math by the third grade, we found, he or she was more likely to be incarcerated later in life. So we offered ourselves as tutors to elementary schools in our community. The principals of the schools were excited that we would present ourselves to meet this need. They were used to churches that wanted to rent spaces for worship and Bible study. They were used to churches that complained that they were failing kids. They were used to churches evangelizing and preaching. They *weren't* used to churches wanting to address a major need of the children in partnership with the schools.

We didn't ask for permission to address this social

issue in our community. Instead, we made an offering of ourselves.

To preach the gospel is to present Jesus Christ as Lord and Savior. It is a call to repentance and the acceptance of Christ's sacrifice for us. But it is more than that. As the Bible demonstrates repeatedly, the gospel is also the proclaiming, in words and deeds, of the Kingdom of God—a right-side-up world. The gospel includes healing the sick, calling out evil spirits, seeing to the poor and the incarcerated, and welcoming the stranger. It is not a stretch to include tutoring children in under-resourced communities and school systems.

Every January, around the time of the national holiday of Dr. Martin Luther King Jr., I find myself reflecting deeply on his work. King gave voice and leadership to a revolutionary movement. One of the key distinctives of his work was that he rooted it in the revolutionary love of Christ Jesus. Many times when Dr. King wanted to provide a picture of the ultimate goal of the Civil Rights Movement, he would refer to the "beloved community"—his language to describe the biblical portrait of God's right-side-up Kingdom. In the beloved community, people across the spectrum of race and class could collectively experience equality, justice, and reconciliation. King's rallies often took place in churches and included prayer, singing, and powerful sermons. King would help people see the connections between following Christ and seeking justice and equality.

Christ is a liberator. We are set free in Christ. The Kingdom of God shows up in us through our acceptance of Christ and the indwelling of the Holy Spirit. But this transformative Kingdom work is not just meant to take place privately within our being. The gospel is demonstrated through the dismantling of broken structures and systems. This is about the Kingdom of God going public.

Justice and intimacy with God should not be pitted against each other, because Christ joins them together. To make the Kingdom of God public and rooted in the revolutionary love of Christ is to wage war against evil and the invisible ruler of this upside-down world.

The Black Lives Matter movement can be viewed in a similar fashion to the Civil Rights Movement. While its ties to the church are less explicit than the Civil Rights Movement, the central question of Black Lives Matter is theological: In the face of evidence to the contrary, do black lives matter? Poor people, marginalized people, even people with a criminal background—do their lives have value?

In an upside-down world, that question is hard to answer. But in a world set right—in the Kingdom of God—the answer is an easy yes. People who are made in the image of God matter. God feels in his gut the plight of people, however harassed and helpless they might be. If we have surrendered to this God, if we have joined the battle to set the world right, will we go with God's gut? Are we willing to wage war against injustice? And what will our weapon of choice be?

We are still living in a time of racial conflict. We still live in a time when violence is seen as the primary solution to conflict. We live in a time when the dignity of every person made in the image of God is under question. There are still people who are in need of liberation and empowerment. There are still people who are held captive by fear. There is still a need for the Kingdom of God to be brought to bear upon injustice, violence, and division. Our weapon of choice is the revolutionary love found in Christ Jesus.

To follow Christ is to follow him into the declaration and demonstration of the Kingdom of God. The church as a collective community of Kingdom laborers takes the Kingdom public. As the lost are found, the hurting are helped, and the captive are liberated, we get a sneak preview of what this upside-down world will look like when it's finally and fully turned right side up.

Of course, to follow Christ is to get into some trouble. To an upside-down world, Christ looks more like a threat than a promise. We have to prepare ourselves for the hard work of love, which is where we turn next.

QUESTIONS FOR REFLECTION AND DISCUSSION

How did you know the first time you were in love?

How have you experienced God's love for you?

What battles are you facing? What battles are you seeing in your community? How can you use love as the weapon of choice in your daily life?

7

TURNING THE WORLD RIGHT SIDE UP

WHEN I WAS A COLLEGE STUDENT, I worked every summer at Park Avenue United Methodist Church, a church in the neighborhood where I grew up. The first two summers I served on the summer day camps team under Kathy Erickson, the children's ministry director. The next summer I thought I was going to serve on the junior high team under Art Erickson (Kathy's husband), the youth ministry director. I was very surprised when Art told me that I would be shadowing him for the summer and leading my own outreach programs.

At the beginning of the summer, Art took me out to breakfast and affirmed what he saw in me as leadership gifts and potential. He also talked about the need for indigenous leaders in urban ministry. He challenged me to connect my gifts and potential with a heart for my city. He told me the story of a Christian leader in the city of Pittsburgh by the name of Reid Carpenter. As I understand the story, Reid became a Kingdom-advancing leader in Pittsburgh because someone who saw his potential challenged him to be a part of making the city as strong for Christ as it was for steel. Art was challenging me in a similar fashion about my own city of Minneapolis.

So that summer Art gave me the responsibility to develop an outreach event in the community and to take leadership over the theme and some of the activities at the middle school summer camp. I must admit that I was nervous, but I was also motivated by Art's belief in my gifts and potential. For the outreach event I decided that I would put on a celebrity basketball game in the community. There was a member of the church named Al Nuness, who was a former pro basketball player in the NBA. At the time he was an executive with the Minnesota Timberwolves, the relatively new NBA team in our town. Al knew a number of former Division I college and NBA players, as well as some former professional football players. There were even some current members of the basketball team of the University of Minnesota who were attending the church and volunteering in the community for the summer. All that was left to do was to ask.

I went to Al's office in downtown Minneapolis, where he worked overseeing marketing for the Timberwolves. I shared with him my vision for the celebrity basketball game. I also shared how Art Erickson had given me leadership responsibilities over this outreach event as well as some of the middle school activities for the summer. To my surprise, Al was excited and very willing to help me—I mean, I was just a young person from South Minneapolis, and yet this former NBA basketball player and current NBA executive was willing to help me with this outreach event.

The church had a large parking lot in the back with two basketball courts. We would have a community 3-on-3 tournament that middle school youth could sign up for. There would be trophies and prizes for the event. There would be a small registration fee so that youth would be committed to show up, but I made sure that money would not keep youth in the community from participating.

Art told me ahead of time what my budget was for the event, but he also let me know that I would have to work with him to raise the money. He took me with him to meet with some Christian businesspeople who also were members of the church. Whenever I was riding in Art's car on the way to meet with someone, he would give me advice about them; after the meeting was over, he would ask me questions on how I could improve my presentation the next time. As we met with these businesspeople, I would share my vision for the celebrity basketball game and 3-on-3 tournament. They liked the idea and committed to support it in various ways.

After I had raised the budget for the event, I put the overall plan together. There would be a 3-on-3 tournament that would start in the morning and conclude with a championship game late in the afternoon. We would provide hamburgers, hot dogs, chips, and soda. That evening the celebrity basketball game would take place; at halftime one of the players would share his testimony on how he became a Christian. Then the player would ask whether any of the young people there would want to give their life to Christ. After that, the celebrity basketball game would finish, and players would stay to hang out with youth and their families.

The day of the event, I went from being nervous to being super-nervous. Even though we had passed out flyers throughout the neighborhood and some kids had preregistered, would people really show up? Would clouds and rain stay away? Would all the celebrity players show up? I stood in the parking lot that morning and asked God to bless the event.

To my excitement and relief, there were positive answers to all of the questions in my nervous head. A lot of youth in the neighborhood showed up to play; others came to cheer on their friends and family members. Even though I recognized some young people from rival gangs, the event remained peaceful. Allen Reid, a former professional football player in the NFL, gave his testimony at the halftime of the celebrity basketball team, and a number of youth came forward to accept Christ into their lives. The event went beyond what I could have imagined. As I watched people leaving later that evening, I saw Art standing across the parking lot, smiling at me.

The next month, we were at the middle school summer camp. The theme was battles that we face in life. We focused on the temptations and challenges that youth face in the inner city and on how one can live a life of character and purpose. To emphasize the theme of a battle I had an idea: another summer staff person and I would have an epic battle in front of the whole camp. I grew up watching and going to pro wrestling matches, and thought a pro wrestling epic championship battle would reinforce the theme in a fun and engaging way. My friend Shawn on the summer staff would be the Urban Warrior; I would be a wrestler named Brown Sugar. We found costumes and theme music. Of course I was the good guy; Shawn's character was evil.

After dinner at camp we had all the youth go out to the playground area to watch us wrestle. I thought it was going well until a number of the middle school boys decided to start having their own battles against each other. Middle school boys were wrestling all over the place; some were out of control. My idea to lift up the theme for the camp, it turns out, didn't go so well.

I felt really bad that night, yet Art found me and encouraged me. He challenged me to learn from that experience but also told me that was just the beginning of the many opportunities I would have to grow as a leader.

That summer in South Minneapolis wasn't the only time I was equipped and empowered for leadership as a youth or young adult. I realize that my leadership of World Impact today is deeply connected to how I was empowered for leadership as an urban young person. Though I didn't feel qualified and I made mistakes, I was given the opportunity to serve as a Kingdom leader and laborer. These experiences developed my passion for the Kingdom of God to come to bear upon the brokenness of urban communities and the sin of racism and racial divisions.

In this upside-down world there is a need for an army of right-side-up people who are committed to advancing the Kingdom of God. This is how love, grace, justice, truth, and reconciliation break through into this broken world. But who is qualified to be a part of the army of Kingdom laborers and leaders?

In this upside-down world there is a heavy emphasis on qualifications that determine whether someone can step into leadership. I don't disagree with the notion of being qualified for a task, role, or assignment. But consider this: In our world today we have a lot of highly qualified people in positions of leadership in various career fields. People in such positions have college degrees, licenses, and certifications. And yet with all these qualified people, our world seems to be getting worse—more violent, more oppressive, more divided, more poverty-stricken. There are more broken families, more incarcerated people. Technical qualifications don't seem to be the answer to more healing, more reconciliation, more peace, more justice, and more transformed lives. You can be a highly qualified person and have an upside-down heart and a lost soul.

Maybe we should explore more deeply the strategy of Christ for raising up an army of right-side-up people. Christ demonstrated the Kingdom of God not just by interacting with qualified people but by empowering the so-called unqualified. Christ initiated a strategy of using the oppressed, the despised, the marginalized, the rebellious, and the outcast to advance God's Kingdom. Christ didn't just feed the hungry multitudes, give sight to the blind, raise the dead, cure the diseased, recognize the full personhood of the outcast, and call evil spirits out of the demonized. He also called such people to follow him and participate in his right-side-up work.

Consider John 4, in which Christ meets with the Samaritan woman at the well, as an example. If there was any group of people that would be unqualified in the eyes of Jewish religious leaders at the time, it would have been Samaritans. Yet Christ had to go to this unqualified location. Why? Because it was connected to his right-side-up work of declaring and demonstrating the Kingdom of God to an upside-down world. An upside-down world doesn't realize it's upside-down until it sees things turned right side up. By qualifying the unqualified, by raising up women and other marginalized people as central to his mission, Christ demonstrated the possibility of a world set right.

One of the ways we can provide a glimpse of the upside-down world being turned right side up is to empower the poor, the marginalized, and the (seemingly) unqualified. Christ spoke of the last becoming first and the first becoming last (Matthew 20:16) as a way to describe the Kingdom of God. When the poor are participating in the fulfillment of the great commission in the same way as the privileged, things are being set right.

Most of the time, visions of successful churches and fruitful Christian living are presented from the perspective of the privileged. Conferences and books focused on planting churches, doing outreach, developing models of discipleship, and engaging justice include inherent assumptions that the reader is part of a privileged class. It's as if the poor have nothing to offer when it comes to advancing the Kingdom of God. How is this different from the elite religious climate and structures that existed when Christ was walking the earth? Don Davis of World Impact often says that the poor should have just as much right to fail as the privileged. And yet the privileged are given the upper hand in the body of Christ. How is this any different from how the upside-down world operates?

Christ was criticized for hanging out with, recognizing the humanity of, and empowering the poor, the incarcerated, the left-for-dead, and the cursed. He saw this unqualified multitude as potential evangelists, prophets, and church planters. The church lives up to its countercultural and right-side-up mandate when it strives to see the poor empowered to participate in the making of disciples and the transformation of communities.

FOLLOWING CHRIST TO THE PLACES OTHERS AVOID

Christ went to a well in Samaria and met with a Samaritan woman there. He went to a place and placed himself in a situation others avoided. Setting things right in this world begins by going to places and into situations that others avoid. In many ways, under-resourced urban and rural communities are the way they are because they have been abandoned and are currently avoided by many. In our world home-lessness, incarceration, and addiction are seen as hopeless causes, quickly abandoned in favor of easier victories. Racial injustice is still an issue because too many people are avoiding engaging it as ambassadors of reconciliation and, as Dr. Martin Luther King Jr. regularly referred to himself, drum majors for justice.

God in the form of Christ goes to the abandoned and avoided places. Christ calls the unqualified— fishermen, Samaritan women, and zealots—to join his army of right-side-up people. In Christ's view, social challenges are opportunities for good news to be revealed, for transformation to occur.

Christ calls the unqualified and qualifies them. Imagine what he can do through us when we refuse to disqualify people, when we have eyes to see trans-formation in every circumstance. When we go to the homeless, the incarcerated, and the addicted with the belief that there can be such transformation in their current circumstance—that they can become right-side-up change agents—we participate in Christ's Kingdom revolution.

When Christ sat at the well and the Samaritan woman arrived, he asked her for a drink of water. This was a strange request, considering the broken rela-tions between men and women, Samaritans and Jews, at the time. But simply by going to this avoided place and asking for a drink from this outcast woman, Christ was dismantling an upside-down and broken system. We often read this encounter through a framework of individualism, featuring one woman meeting with Christ for her individual life transformation. But this reading of the story is a very limited understanding of the gospel. Yes, this meeting with Christ would challenge her life, but so would an upside-down system that marginalized women. The Samaritan woman lets us in on this truth: It went against the custom of the time or system, she reminded Jesus, for her to be having such a conversation across ethnicity and gender. It's not just that Christ goes into the avoided places, but how he goes. He sits down and asks for a drink.

When we look at the marginalized, outcast, and oppressed, it's easy to just focus on what we can do for them. But even highly qualified people with upside-down hearts are able to feel pity and mercy for the less fortunate. The right-side-up people of the Kingdom of God are able to humble themselves before the less fortunate, believing that they can be blessed by them and not just be a blessing. By taking this posture we become countercultural people in this world.

We don't just take a posture of humility and await a blessing in avoided places. There are also blessings awaiting us, and Kingdom work for us to do, in relation to uncomfortable situations and issues that people tend to want to avoid. How can we enter conflict with humility and the expectation of blessing?

Our default mode for entering conflict—if we enter it at all—includes pride, arrogance, selfishness, and even violence. We may enter into conflict with past wounds, a dysfunctional spirit of blame, and prejudices. What if we made a commitment to enter into conflict with humility, grace, love, and a teachable spirit? What if we entered into each conflict expecting a blessing of forgiveness, reconciliation, and transformation? Such expectation and commitments would seem completely upside-down to people accustomed to life in a broken world, but in the Kingdom of God such expectations and commitments are normal and good.

When Christ entered Samaria, he was entering into a space of conflict, brokenness, and tension. He entered that space as the embodiment of God's revolutionary love and reconciliation. How do we enter this upside-down world every day? Who and what do we really represent? Each day is a new opportunity to enter a broken world on behalf of God and God's Kingdom. It's important to spend intimate time with God, to set our hearts right, so that out of the overflow of that relationship we each may enter into this world as someone other. We enter the broken spaces of this world not of our own accord. We enter representing an agenda beyond our own. We enter out of obedience to our heavenly Father, who longs to turn our world right side up.

This posture of humility and the awaiting of blessing is also what we must bring into the challenging issue of race, racial division, and racism. It's what will deal with the lingering and continual impact of privilege and victimization. As ambassadors of reconciliation, we have a missional obligation to enter into this broken space. But we can't enter this space expecting the Kingdom of God to show up if we enter with sustained anger, bitterness, ignorance, arrogance, unforgiveness, and privilege. Racial division and injustice are killing us. Lives are literally being lost because of how race and racism function in this upside-down world. This evil force kills our ability to communicate, reconcile, and develop harmonious community.

We must come into this upside-down space as listeners, learners, and with repentant hearts. This is where we can again allow God to kill us softly, re-creating us as ambassadors of reconciliation (2 Corinthians 5:18-19). God can open our eyes to how multiethnic and multicultural the Bible is. God can lead us into encounters with churches culturally different from the ones we grew up in or currently attend. As we allow God to do this soul surgery on us, our lives will be recalibrated to accommodate a more diverse community.

FOLLOWING CHRIST INTO A NEW IDENTITY AND WORSHIP

For these transformations to take root, we will need to repent. We must acknowledge the ways in which we participate in the upside-down world. When, for example, we are confronted with the existence of individual and systemic racism or with the ways in which prejudice and stereotyping show up in our own hearts and minds, we can get defensive. When confronted with the prevalence of racism, some people feel they are being accused of being a racist. The way forward is to allow God to work on us and to lead people into our lives who build us up in the right-side-up image of God.

We have struggled mightily around the issue of race in the United States, whether dealing with racial disparities in employment, education, home ownership, and incarceration; processing the number of deaths of unarmed African Americans at the hands of police officers; or bemoaning the murder of police officers. As an African American I have navigated challenges in my community related to the devaluing of our own lives through a racialized self-hate: gang violence, the oppression of African American women, and the devaluing of life in the womb. White brothers and sisters often refuse to acknowledge the real and sinful forces of racial privilege, racial profiling, and systemic racial oppression fueling the racial divide. And generally speaking, we collectively continue to think of racial dysfunction as primarily a black-white issue, marginalizing the concerns and experiences of Asians, Hispanics, and other ethnic groups. We tend to not want to discuss a whole list of issues that divide ethnic groups, such as immigration. Christians have to being willing to die to ideologies that clash with the right-side-up world envisioned in the Scriptures, to die to our self-understandings that clash with our identity in Christ. The Kingdom of God can be brought to bear on any issue, no matter how delicate or volatile, if we are willing to enter into the issue with humility and courage and love. When we do so, we follow Christ.

It is possible to accept Christ as Lord and Savior and still accept an upside-down place and space in this world. How can this happen? We turn God and Christ upside down when we subject them to our social constructs—race, political ideology, and so on. When our proclamations and portrayals of Christ are based on the upside-down social constructs of this world, then our understanding of God and our gospel witness are compromised. We are still held captive to our upside-down world. We need to turn around—to be turned around.

When Christ met the Samaritan woman at the well and began a conversation, she was bewildered. She questioned what a Jewish man was doing talking with her. She acknowledged the social norm that Christ was challenging. What she saw as normal and appropriate for her, however, was actually upside-down space, and what she saw as upside-down actions were actually

Christ turning her right side up. We will never understand our true place in this world as Kingdom citizens and beloved children of God until we realize we are navigating upside-down space. In comparison to the Kingdom of God, every man-made structure and system is at some level limited and upside-down. Without my life being regenerated by a Savior sent by God, my life is upside-down—and so is my world.

The encounter between Christ and the Samaritan woman was so other-worldly that it led to her realization of a new identity and a new worship. She let Christ softly kill her upside-down self, and then he resurrected her into a right-side-up way of life.

Like the Samaritan woman, we must allow God into the deep places of our identities. Our ultimate goal here is transformation and new life in the Kingdom of God. This includes both individual life-change (dying to our old selves and individual sins) and systemic transformation (our rejection of and participation in the dismantling of unjust, unbiblical systems). The Kingdom of God transforms every life, community, and system it enters. Where the Kingdom of God is not being realized, we should consider to what extent we are participating in a limited or contaminated version of the gospel.

Christ mentioned to the Samaritan woman that she had been married multiple times and was living with a man she wasn't married to. He did not ignore her individual circumstances when he confronted the separation of Jews and Samaritans. Both of these issues represented cultural breakdown, then and now. The issues of race and broken families today are both individual challenges and systemic issues. We make a mistake when we think of the Samaritan woman's story as solely an individual's issues and not the issues of society. The breakdown of individuals, as we saw at the beginning of this book, is interwoven with the breakdown of society.

Some people, for example, try to address each instance of racial tension or conflict into an isolated event, not connected to any other incident. To do so goes against how the Bible deals with ethnic divisions: Christ addresses the Samaritan woman not just as an individual but as a representative of an ethnic group in long-standing and complex conflict with his own ethnic group. In our day, I have been a victim of racial profiling, and I've learned over the years that I'm not the only one—I'm not the only African American to be pulled over by the police for no good reason. Many others have experienced the same thing. My experience of racial profiling is not an individual issue; it's a systemic issue. And because this systemic issue is connected to law enforcement, that makes it an institutional issue. And because this systemic issue plays out in individual encounters, it has an impact on the lives and souls of individuals.

Similarly, divorce is an issue that impacts many individuals, but it's not just an individual issue. You can probably isolate specific reasons why particular people have gone through a divorce. At the same time, when you look at divorce rates in the United States, you cannot avoid the conclusion that it is a broader systemic issue, impacting the lives of many people, including children and youth. Christ brought up the Samaritan woman's relationship history—including her being divorced five times—for her own personal transformation, but not simply for that reason. Why would Christ's conversation with the Samaritan woman swing so wildly back and forth between her personal life and the cultural division between Jews and Samaritans? Because her series of relationships represented a bigger pattern, an upside-down system.

In general, when it came to marriage and divorce in the time of Jesus, the male was in the position of power. A young man could go to the father of the woman he wanted to marry, and they would pretty much decide how things were going to go. The woman had some say in the matter, but not at the same level as the man. Similarly, a man could divorce a woman based on a number of things that made the woman come across as being the only one at fault. The woman was a second-class citizen in this upside-down gender space.

So while this conversation would have been uncomfortable for the Samaritan woman, we can't just paint the scene as a woman being embarrassed by her indiscretions. Her predicament also had to do with her place in a system of gender dysfunction that traced back to the original sin in the Garden of Eden. Christ confronted it and killed it with a declaration of good news, and the woman became an agent of transformation for her whole community.

In order to experience a greater realization of the Kingdom of God in this upside-down world, we need to deal with the uncomfortable issues both in our personal lives and within the systems and institutions around us. Christ brings the Samaritan woman's personal brokenness to light; he also exposes the brokenness of her society across ethnic, gender, and even religious lines. The separation of Jews and Samaritans by where and how they worshiped reveals the ultimate depth of their systemic separation. But Christ describes a time when they will not be separated by who they are in terms of gender or ethnicity, or where and how they worship. Christ casts a vision to the Samaritan woman of a world set right, when Jews and Samaritans will worship together under a new identity, rooted in truth and empowered by the Spirit.

This is the kind of worship God desires. To live into this now is to live out a sneak preview of the eternal Kingdom to come and to experience the blessing of the Kingdom today. When we enter into upside-down spaces and engage people living under wrongful labels, enslaved to a broken world, we can point to the possibility of a new identity in Christ: a right-side-up people from every tongue and tribe and nation. When people embrace this new identity and go out from such reconciled worship into a broken world, they go as an army of the Kingdom of God, and the gates of hell will not prevail.

FOLLOWING CHRIST INTO A REVOLUTIONARY MOVEMENT

The encounter the Samaritan woman had with Christ was so powerful and transformative that she forgot why she had come to the well in the first place. She left her water pot, and empowered by the "living water" that came from Christ, she ran into town to tell others about her encounter with him. The revolutionary movement she ignited was empowered with a new life mission. She was no longer being led primarily by the upside-down identity of a marginalized woman, divorced five times, living sinfully with her boyfriend. She was a new creation, following Christ into a revolutionary movement.

A revolt is about taking your allegiance from one leader or government and giving it to another. You once found your identity in one systemic or cultural way of living; now you have surrendered yourself to a new system, with different values and cultural ways of living. Having come to the realization that Jesus was the Messiah, the Samaritan woman decided that she wanted to surrender to the mission of the Kingdom he represented. And she was ready to go into town and publicly tell everyone about her new allegiance. This is revolutionary living: You are so overcome and transformed by an encounter with Christ that you can't keep it to yourself. You desire to go and tell others about Christ, and lead them to him so that they can be transformed as well.

To go into town with this bold message went against the Samaritan woman's place in her upside-down society. A woman was not supposed to teach men, especially not a woman whose personal life was so scandalous. She broke the social rules of the day by becoming an evangelist to her town, and in so doing she found her rightful place as a right-side-up person in an upside-down world. This was an empowering demonstration of the Kingdom of God. A marginalized, corrupted, sinful, and second-class person became a leader. This is the good news of the Kingdom of God: Christ reveals the world set-right through the empowerment of the marginalized.

When we allow God to kill us softly, we may experience discomfort because our upside-down identities are embedded deep within us. But we also receive the liberation of a new identity and life mission. God meets us at the well of our circumstances, stresses, and doubts, skillfully takes us through his soul surgery, and makes us rise up again, to share the transforming power of God wherever we find ourselves. This is the Christian life: participation in the revolutionary movement of Christ. Our life rhythm becomes one of regularly meeting with Christ, following Christ into our upside-down world, and giving witness to the world set right so that individual lives and whole communities might be transformed.

As we meet with God at the wells of our lives, we realize not only that we are beloved of God but also that we are God's solution to communities in need. We can no longer simply complain or opine about what someone should do about the problems in our city or town. God has commissioned you and me, his beloved children, as the solution to the upside-down conditions that surround us. We are called to be salt and light where there is bitterness and darkness. God will speak into our lives in ways that empower us to rise up in such a time as this.

As a Christian, someone whom God has killed softly and then resurrected as a new creation, you are qualified for this work. Many ordinary, everyday Christians doubt this. We have limited our imaginations to think that having a public impact for the Kingdom of God is only for those preaching, leading worship, or growing a church. But the Kingdom of God will be advanced in this upside-down world as ordinary Christians rise up to do extraordinary works in public places. That's where the need is: The Kingdom must come to bear in public schools, small businesses, community centers, hospitals, and the arts. These places don't necessarily need a preacher or a worship leader. They need reconcilers, storytellers, healers, listeners, servants, and burden-bearers. The harvest is plentiful, and God's love is powerful enough to make Kingdom laborers of each of us. The question is whether our hearts are open enough to answer the call.

Our hesitancy can be rooted in our not knowing where to begin or what to do. We will have to trust God in new ways. Our rising up will come out of the overflow of our prioritizing time with God. The more we spend time with God, the more clarity he will give us on the ways in which the Kingdom will come to bear on our particular place or situation. You may not sense clarity from every single time alone with God, but that's okay. This, too, is how God kills us softly. He does soul-surgery on us, and while we may not hear an audible voice of God saying, "Go here" or "Do this," God's love will guide and direct us. Christ didn't say to the Samaritan woman, "Go into town and tell everyone about me." Her encounter with Christ did something so deep inside her that she was moved to rise up from the well, leave her position in an upside-down society, and tell others the good news about him. Simply by offering time alone to God, we invite him to do something so empowering within us that we rise up and go proclaim his right-side-up Kingdom to our upside-down world.

This is discipleship: being equipped and empowered to live out the great commission in tangible ways. In a right-side-up world, discipleship is not limited to a special class of people. Why can't a homeless person become an evangelist? Why can't the incarcerated claim their prisons or county jails as a mission field? Why can't a welfare mother become a church planter? Why can't you be the solution to a problem that exists at your job, at your school, or in your community? All that and more is possible when the people of God recognize that they are dearly loved by God and are citizens of his Kingdom, endowed with his mission.

Following Christ in an upside-down world is about stepping away from upside-down identities, behaviors, and systems in order to live in God's right-side-up Kingdom. We are God's beloved children, Kingdom citizens, and ambassadors of reconciliation. To the people still enslaved by the broken systems and structures of this world, our way of life seems utterly upside down. But we have been turned around, and the experience of being killed softly by God and born again into the right-side-up life in his Kingdom makes us passionate, desperate, to liberate and empower the world around us—to join God's mission to set the whole world right.

QUESTIONS FOR REFLECTION AND DISCUSSION

How has God met you at the well of your life?

How have you experienced God changing your view of yourself?

Where is there an opportunity for you to rise up as God's agent of transformation in your world?

About the Author

EFREM SMITH'S personal and professional story paints a compelling picture of an urban church leader of deep faith. Throughout his career—leading Christian community development efforts; serving as a pastor, church planter, and leader in the Evangelical Covenant Church; and now serving as president and CEO of World Impact—Efrem has had a passion for the urban poor, theological education, and training indigenous leaders for service in the Kingdom.

As a preacher, motivational speaker, and author, Efrem Smith is internationally recognized for his passion to see lasting life transformations, communities revitalized to reach the marginalized, and further Kingdom advancement within our churches.

Efrem has been a keynote speaker for such events as Athletes in Action, Campus Crusade for Christ, Youth Specialties, Compassion International, Thrive, and more. He is the author of *Raising Up Young Heroes*,

The Hip-Hop Church, Jump, and *The Post-Black and Post-White Church.*

Efrem is the recipient of many awards, such as the Role Model Award from the Hennepin County Community Coalition and the Community Service Award from Saint John's University. He is a graduate of Saint John's University and Luther Theological Seminary and is currently completing his doctorate in church leadership from Bethel Seminary. He and his wife, Donecia, along with their two children, Jeada and Mireya, live in the San Francisco Bay Area.